THE BOOK THAT HAS TAKEN THE COUNTRY BY STORM

THE AMITYVILLE HORROR

"I stared into the mirror in sheer disbelief. 'That's not me! That can't be me!' I screamed. I, Kathleen Lutz, am a young blonde-haired housewife with pale soft skin—but that's not what I saw in my reflection. I had turned into a disgusting-looking 90-year-old hag! My hair was white and scraggly. Ugly creases and crow's feet scarred my face. I drooled all over my shriveled up, dried skin. It was the work of horrible evil spirits that plunged my family and me into chilling terror for 28 days . . . that turned our dream house into a hell house."

TURN THE PAGE AND NOW, GO ON WITH THE STORY!

SAMUEL Z. ARKOFF
PRESENTS

JAMES BROLIN

MARGOT KIDDER

ROD STEIGER

In

THE AMITYVILLE HORROR

Also Starring
MURRAY HAMILTON

Music by
LALO SCHIFRIN

Executive in Charge of Production
JERE HENSHAW

Executive Producer
SAMUEL Z. ARKOFF

Screenplay by
SANDOR STERN

Based on the Book by
JAY ANSON

Produced by
RONALD SALAND and ELLIOT GEISINGER

Directed by
STUART ROSENBERG

A PROFESSIONAL FILMS, INC. PRODUCTION
A CINEMA 77 FILM
RELEASED BY AMERICAN INTERNATIONAL

THE AMITYVILLE HORROR

BY JAY ANSON

BANTAM BOOKS
TORONTO · NEW YORK · LONDON

THE AMITYVILLE HORROR

*A Bantam Book / published by arrangement with
Prentice-Hall, Inc.*

PRINTING HISTORY

*Prentice-Hall edition published July 1977
13 printings through March 1978*

Bantam edition / August 1978

2nd printing ____August 1978	10th printing ____August 1978
3rd printing ____August 1978	11th printing _September 1978
4th printing ____August 1978	12th printing _September 1978
5th printing ____August 1978	13th printing ____October 1978
6th printing ____August 1978	14th printing _December 1978
7th printing ____August 1978	15th printing _December 1978
8th printing ____August 1978	16th printing ____January 1979
9th printing ____August 1978	17th printing ___February 1979

Bantam movie edition / July 1979

ISBN 0-553-13160-5

CONTENTS

PREFACE
by Reverend John Nicola

The problem to which this book addresses itself is one which, although it is as old as mankind, needs to be brought to the attention of thoughtful readers today. All civilizations have expressed some sense of insecurity and fear over the spotty but recurring reports of phenomena that leave men feeling victimized by hostile beings with superhuman powers. Human beings in different societies have responded to such challenges in various ways. Words, gestures, and amulets or other objects have been ritually employed in response to demonic attacks; this was as true of the ancient Semitic civilizations like the Babylonians and their feared Udug demons as it is of present Christian rites of exorcism.

In our modern Western world, there are three main stances which, in various combinations, characterize the multitude of attitudes individuals assume toward reports of siege by mysterious powers. The first, the *scientific*, views the world—and perhaps the universe—as governed by unvarying laws that have been discovered, or at least are discoverable, by scientific investigation. Diametrically opposed to this is a stance that seems to deplore, if not ignore, the findings of science seeing empirical reality as shallow and meaningless; it focuses instead on unseen spiritual realities, and may be characterized as *superstitious*. The third stance contains something of each of the other two. While adhering to science as a method, it broadens the vistas of positive science, incorporating spiritual dimensions of reality through theological and philosophical considerations. This we may call the *religious* stance.

One certainty is that the phenomena reported in this book do happen—and to ordinary people and families who are neither exhibitionists or attention seekers. Often the response of the positive scientist is to deny the reality of reported data and to refuse even to examine the evidence; here, it appears, we are dealing with a prejudice. On the other hand, those scientists who credit the evidence and apply scientific methodology to attempting an explanation generally restrict the possibilities to science as it is known today, or presume that projected findings of empirical science will one day explain the phenomena. This is one reasonable and integral approach.

Superstitious people seize on psychic phenomena as justification for a sometimes unreasonable approach to life. Interjecting irrational fears and senseless preconceived notions or explanations into situations like the

Amityville case Jay Anson describes here simply increases the suffering of those involved. The prejudice thus exhibited is clear.

Needless to say, incorporated in a religiously oriented person's point of view are the data of revelation. Since revelation presumes communication from God, and in turn presumes the existence of God and His interest in human affairs, we can see that here, too, a prejudice is implied—to wit, the prejudice of faith. The balanced person of faith will admire and accept the findings of modern science but conclude that, even projecting future developments, it is myopic to think that nature does not reveal a depth of reality beyond the empirical realm of natural science. As is the case with an open-minded scientist, a sensible believer may also accept an integrated approach to psychic phenomena.

Thus we observe that whatever stance an individual adopts, it will rest on certain prejudices that cannot be proven to the satisfaction of those who choose to adopt a different construction. When psychic phenomena occur in the life of a family, and that family looks for help, its members may be repelled equally by the naïveté of the superstitious, the uncertainty of those who profess belief in the supernatural but seem ashamed and confused at their own beliefs, and by the haughty pride of the positive scientist asserting with certainty things contradictory to one's own experience.

Unfortunately, this complex web of ignorance, bias, and fear causes a great deal of suffering for the unsuspecting family suddenly tossed into an upsetting and frightening situation. It is just such a case to which Jay Anson addresses himself. If the story were fiction, it would easily be dismissed as irrelevant. It is, however, a documentary told by the family and the priest who actually experienced what is reported; and as such, the tale must give us pause for thought. Those of us who have been involved in psychic investigations can verify the fact that the case is not atypical.

Because of the uncertainties connected with the paranormal, I, as a believer in science and in religion, would be remiss not to warn readers against the dangers both of an arrogance that professes a grasp of the unknown and of a bravado that boasts a control of the transcendent. The wise man knows that he does *not* know —and the prudent man respects what he does not control.

THE
AMITYVILLE
HORROR

PROLOGUE

On February 5, 1976, the *Ten O'Clock News* on New York's Channel Five announced it was doing a series on people who claimed to have extrasensory powers. The program cut to reporter Steve Bauman investigating an allegedly haunted house in Amityville, Long Island.

Bauman said that on November 13, 1974, a large colonial house at 112 Ocean Avenue had been the scene of a mass murder. Twenty-four-year-old Ronald DeFeo had taken a high-powered rifle and methodically shot to death his parents, two brothers, and two sisters. DeFeo had subsequently been sentenced to life imprisonment.

"Two months ago," the report continued, "the house was sold for $80,000 to a couple named George and Kathleen Lutz." The Lutzes had been aware of the killings, but not being superstitious, they had felt the house would be perfect for themselves and their three children.

They moved in on December 18. Shortly thereafter, Bauman said, they had become aware that the place was inhabited by some psychic force and that they feared for their lives. "They talked of feeling the presence of some energy inside, some unnatural evil that grew stronger each day they remained."

Four weeks after they moved in, the Lutzes abandoned the house, taking only a few changes of clothes. At present, they were staying with friends in an undisclosed location. But before they left, Channel Five stated, their predicament had become known in the area. They had consulted the police and a local priest as well as a psychic research group. "They reportedly told of strange voices seeming to come from within themselves, of a power which actually lifted Mrs. Lutz off her feet toward a closet behind which was a room not noted on any blueprints."

Reporter Steve Bauman had heard of their claims. After doing some background research on the house, he discovered that tragedy had struck nearly every family inhabiting the place, as well as an earlier house built on the same site.

The Channel Five announcer went on to say that William Weber, the attorney representing Ronald De-Feo, had commissioned studies hoping to prove that some force influenced the behavior of anyone living at 112 Ocean Avenue. Weber claimed this force "may be of natural origin," and felt it might be the evidence he needed to win his client a new trial. On camera, Weber said he was "aware that certain houses could be built or constructed in a certain manner so as to create some sort of electrical currents through some rooms, based on the physical structure of the house. Again, the scientists said they 'are investigating that, to rule that out.' And after they rule out all reasonable or scientific explanation, then it's going to be referred over to another group at Duke University, who will delve into the psychic aspects of the case."

The report concluded by saying that the Catholic Church was also involved. Channel Five stated that two emissaries from the Vatican had arrived in Amityville in December, and were reported to have told the Lutzes to leave their home immediately. "Now the Church's Council of Miracles is studying the case, and its report is that indeed 112 Ocean Avenue is possessed of some spirits beyond current human knowledge."

Two weeks after the telecast, George and Kathy Lutz held a press conference in attorney William Weber's office. The DeFeo lawyer had met the couple three weeks before through mutual friends.

George Lutz stated to reporters that he would not spend another night in the house, but he was not planning to sell 112 Ocean Avenue just then. He was also awaiting the results of some scientific tests to be conducted by parapsychologists and other "sensitive" professional researchers of occult phenomena.

At that point in time, the Lutzes cut off all communication with the media, feeling that too much was being overstated and exaggerated. It is only now that their whole story is being told.

1 December 18, 1975 — George and Kathy Lutz moved into 112 Ocean Avenue on December 18. Twenty-eight days later, they fled in terror.

George Lee Lutz, 28, of Deer Park, Long Island, had a pretty good idea of land and home values. The owner of a land surveying company, William H. Parry, Inc., he proudly let everyone know that the business was a third-generation operation: his grandfather's, his father's, and now his.

Between July and November, he and his wife, Kathleen, 30, had looked at over fifty homes on the Island's

South Shore before deciding to investigate Amityville. None in the thirty to fifty thousand dollar range had yet met their requirements—that the house must be on the water and that it must be one to which they could move George's business.

In the course of their search, George called the Conklin Realty Office in Massapequa Park and spoke to broker Edith Evans. She said that she had a new house that she wanted to show them, and that she could take them through the place between three and three-thirty. George made the appointment and the broker—an attractive, warm woman—took them there at three in the afternoon.

She was very pleasant and patient with the young couple. "I'm not sure if this is what you're looking for," she told George and Kathy, "but I wanted to show you how the 'other half' of Amityville lives."

The house at 112 Ocean Avenue is a big, rambling, three-story affair, with dark shingles and white trim. The lot on which it stands is 50 by 237, the fifty feet facing the front, so that as you look at the house from across the street, the entrance door is down the right side. With the property comes thirty feet of wooden bulkhead that stands against the Amityville River.

On a lamppost at the end of the paved driveway, is a small sign bearing the name given the house by a previous owner. It reads "High Hopes."

An enclosed porch with wet bar looks out at a pre-ferred, older residential community of other big homes. Evergreens grow around the narrow grounds, partly blocking off the neighbors on either side, but their drawn shades can be seen easily enough. When he looked around, George thought that was peculiar. He noticed the neighbors' shades were all drawn on the

8

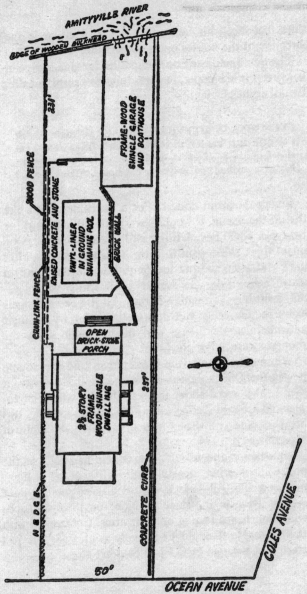

Diagram of the Property, Based on a 1975 Survey

sides that faced his house, but not in front or in the direction of the houses on the other side.

The house had been on the market for almost a year. It was not in the paper, but was fully described in Edith Evans' agency listing:

> **EXCLUSIVE AMITYVILLE AREA—6 bedroom Dutch Colonial, spacious living room, formal dining room, enclosed porch, 3-1/2 baths, finished basement, 2-car garage, heated swimming pool and large boathouse. Asking $80,000**

Eighty thousand dollars! For a house described like that in the listing, it would have to be falling apart, or the typist could have left out a "1" before the "8." One might think she'd want to show a suspect bargain after dark and from the outside only, but she was glad to show them inside. The Lutzes' examination was pleasant, swift but thorough. Not only did it meet with their exact requirements and desires, but contrary to their anticipations, the house and other buildings on the property were in fine condition.

Without hesitation, the broker then told the couple it was the DeFeo house. Everyone in the country, it seems, had heard about the tragedy, the twenty-three-year-old Ronald DeFeo killing his father, mother, two brothers, and two sisters in their sleep on the night of November 13, 1974.

Newspaper and television accounts had told of the police discovering the six bodies all shot by a high-powered rifle. All—as the Lutzes learned months later —were lying in the same position: on their stomachs with their heads resting on their arms. Confronted with this massacre, Ronald had finally confessed: "It just started; it went so fast, I just couldn't stop."

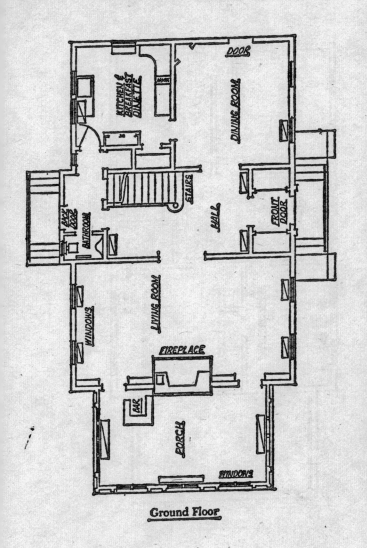

Ground Floor

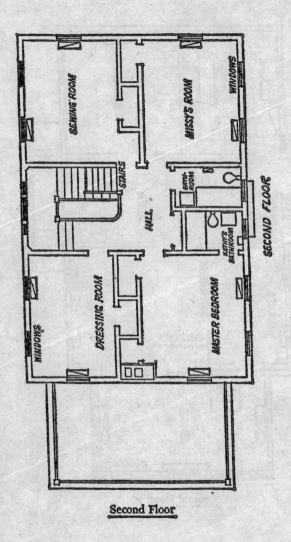

Second Floor

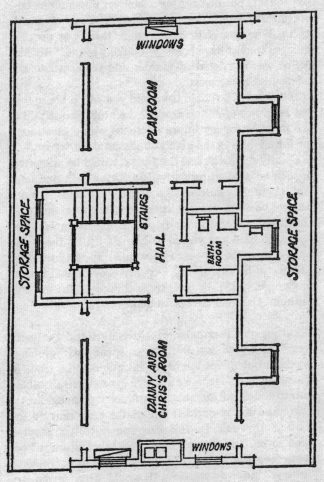

Third Floor/Attic

During his trial, his court-appointed attorney, William Weber, pleaded for his insanity. "For months before the incident," the young man testified, "I heard voices. Whenever I looked around, there was no one there, so it must have been God talking to me." Ronald DeFeo was convicted of murder and sentenced to six consecutive life terms.

"I wonder if I should have told you which house this was *before* or *after* you saw it," the broker mused. "I'd like to know for my future reference with clients looking for a house in the ninety-thousand dollar range."

Clearly she didn't feel the Lutzes would be interested in such an affluent property. But Kathy took one final look about the house, smiled happily and said, "It's the best we've seen. It's got everything we ever wanted." Obviously she had never hoped to live in such a fine house. But George vowed to himself that if there was a way, this was the place he wanted his wife to have. The tragic history of 112 Ocean Avenue didn't matter to George, Kathy, or their three children. This was still the home they had always wanted.

During the remainder of November and the early weeks of December, the Lutzes spent their evenings laying out plans for minor modifications to be made in the new house. George's surveying experience enabled him to rough out suitable layouts for the changes.

He and Kathy decided one of the bedrooms on the third floor would be for their two boys, Christopher aged seven, and Daniel, nine. The other upstairs bedroom they gave to their children as a playroom. Melissa, "Missy," the five-year-old girl, would sleep on the second floor, across the hall from the master bedroom. There would also be a sewing room and a big dressing room for George and Kathy on the same floor. Chris, Danny, and Missy were well pleased with their room assignments.

Downstairs, on the main floor, the Lutzes had a slight problem. They didn't own any dining room furniture. They finally decided that before the closing, George would tell the broker they'd like to purchase the dining room set left in storage by the DeFeos, along with a girl's bedroom set for Missy, a TV chair and Ronald DeFeo's bedroom furniture. These things and other furnishings left in the house, like the DeFeo's bed, were not included in the purchase price. George paid out an additional $400 for these items. He also got for free seven air-conditioners, two washers, two dryers, and a new refrigerator and a freezer.

There was a lot to be accomplished before moving day. In addition to the physical move of all their belongings, there were complicated legal questions, relative to the transfer of the title, that required sifting and sorting out. The title to the house and property was recorded in the names of Ronald DeFeo's parents. It seemed Ronald, as the sole survivor, was entitled to inherit his parents' estate, regardless of the fact that he had been convicted of murdering them. None of the assets in the estate could be disposed of before being legally settled in Probate Court. It was a difficult legal maze that the executors had to travel, and more time was still needed to provide the proper legal administration of any transaction related to the house or property.

The Lutzes were advised that provisions could be devised to protect the legal interests of all concerned if the sale of the house was consummated; but to arrive at the proper procedure to accomplish this could take weeks or longer. Eventually it was resolved that, for the closing, $40,000 was to be put in escrow for the mortgage until a legal deed could be completed and executed.

The closing date was set for the morning George and Kathy planned to move from Deer Park. They had arranged to close on the sale of their old house the day before. Confident that everything could be worked out, and probably influenced by their anxiety to get settled in their new home, the couple decided to try and get everything done on the same day.

Packing was to be mainly Kathy's job. To keep the children out of her hair and away from George, she assigned them minor projects. They would gather their own toys and arrange their clothing for packing. When the chores were completed, they were to start cleaning their rooms to make their old house presentable for the scrutiny of new owners.

George planned to close his office in Syosset and move it into the new house to save on the rent money. He had included this item in his original estimate of how he and Kathy could afford an $80,000 house. Now he figured that the basement, a well-finished layout, might be the best place. Moving his equipment and furnishings would be time consuming enough, and if the basement was to be the location of the new office, some carpentry would be needed.

The 45 by 22 foot boathouse, out behind the house and garage, was not there just to be ostentatious and an unused decoration for the Lutzes. George owned a twenty-five-foot cabin cruiser and a fifteen-foot speedboat. The facilities at his new house would again save him a lot of money he normally had been paying to a marina. The task of getting his vessels to Amityville with a trailer became an obsession with him, despite the priorities that he and Kathy were constantly discovering.

There was work to be done at 112 Ocean Avenue, both inside and outside. Although he wasn't sure where the time was going to come from, George planned to attend to some of the landscaping and the garden to prevent frost damage, maybe put framed burlap around the shrubs, put in bulbs and after that, spread some lime on the lawn.

Handy with his tools and equipment, George made good progress on many interior projects. Now and then, pressed for time, he got his hopeful projects confused with his musts. He soon dropped everything to clean the chimney, then the fireplace. After all, Christmas was coming up.

It was quite cold on the actual moving day. The family had packed the night before and slept on the floor. George was up early and singlehandedly piled the first full load into the biggest U-haul trailer he could rent, finishing in barely enough time to clean up and get to the closing with Kathy.

At the legal ritual, the attorneys used up more than their usually allotted heretos, whereases and parties of, and dealt each other long sheets of typewritten paper. The Lutzes' lawyer explained that because of the impediments on the house, they did not have a clear title to the property, though they'd have the best that could be fashioned for their mortgage. But remarkably, the closing was all over a few minutes past noon. As they rushed from the office, their lawyers assured them they would have no problem and eventually would get proper ownership papers.

At one o'clock, George rolled into the driveway of 112 Ocean Avenue, with the trailer crowded with their belongings, and the DeFeos' refrigerator, washer, dryer and freezer that had been in storage. Kathy followed with the children in the family van with their motorcycle in the back. Five of George's friends, young men in their twenties and husky enough to help move bulky items, were waiting. Furniture, boxes, crates, barrels, bags, toys, bikes, motorcycles, and clothing were taken from the truck onto the patio at the rear of the house and into the garage.

Then George walked to the front door, fumbling in his pockets as he went, searching for the key to the door. Irritated, he returned to the truck and thoroughly searched it before admitting to his assistants that he didn't have it. The broker was the only one with the key, and she had taken it with her as she left the closing. George called her, and she went back to her office to fetch it.

When the side door was finally open, the three children leaped from the van, made right for their respective toys and began a parade of unprofessional movers in and out of the house. Kathy designated the destination of each parcel.

It took time to maneuver furniture up the fairly narrow stairwell leading to the second and third floors. And by the time Father Mancuso arrived to bless the house, it was well after one-thirty P.M.

2 December 18 — Father Frank Mancuso is not only a cleric. In addition to properly attending to his priestly duties, he handles clients in family counseling for his diocese.

That morning, Father Mancuso had woken up feeling uneasy. Something was bothering him. He couldn't put his finger on it, because he really didn't have any particular worries. In his own words, looking back, he can only explain it as a "bad feeling."

All that morning, the priest moved around his apartment in the Long Island rectory in a daze. Today is Thursday, he thought to himself. I've got a lunch date in Lindenhurst, then I must go and bless the Lutzes' new home and be at my mother's for dinner.

Father Mancuso had met George Lee Lutz two years earlier. Even though George was a Methodist, he had helped Kathy and George in the days before they were married. The three children were Kathy's from a previous marriage, and as a priest to Catholic children, Father Mancuso felt a personal need to look after their interests.

The young couple had often asked the friendly cleric with the neatly-trimmed beard to come for lunch or dinner at their home in Deer Park. Somehow that anticipated meeting had never come off. Now, George had a very special reason to invite him anew: Would he come to Amityville to bless their new house? Father Mancuso said he'd be there on December 18.

On the same day he agreed to come to George's house, he also made a date to lunch with four old friends in Lindenhurst, Long Island. His very first parish had been there. Now he was very well regarded in the diocese, with his own quarters at the rectory in Long Island. Understandably he was always busy and held to a hectic schedule, so he could not be blamed for trying to kill two birds with one stone, since Lindenhurst and Amityville were but a few miles apart.

The cleric could not shake the "bad feeling" that persisted even through the pleasant luncheon with his four old acquaintances. However, he kept stalling his leaving for Amityville, pushing ahead the time to go. His friends asked him where he was off to.

"To Amityville."

"Where in Amityville?"

"It's a young couple in their thirties, with three children. They live on . . ." Father Mancuso referred to a slip of paper. "112 Ocean Avenue."

"That's the DeFeo house," one of his friends said.

"No. Their name is Lutz. George and Kathleen Lutz."

"Don't you remember the DeFeos, Frank?" asked one of the men at the table. "Last year? The son killed his whole family. His father, mother, and four brothers and sisters. Terrible, terrible thing. It was a big story in all the papers."

The priest tried to think back. He seldom read the news when he picked up a paper, only looking for items of special interest. "No, I really don't seem to recall it."

Of the four men at the table, three were priests and they somehow didn't like the idea. The consensus was that he shouldn't go.

"I must. I promised them I'd come."

As Father Mancuso drove the few miles to Amityville, he felt apprehensive. It wasn't the fact that he would be visiting the DeFeo house, he was sure, but something else. . . .

It was past one-thirty when he arrived. The Lutzes' driveway was so cluttered that he had to park his old tan Ford on the street. It was an enormous house, he noted. Good for Kathy and the children that her husband had been able to provide such a fine home!

The priest removed his clerical articles from the car, put on his stole, took the holy water, and entered the house to begin his ritual of blessing. When he flicked the first holy water and uttered the words that accompany the gesture, Father Mancuso heard a masculine voice say with terrible clarity: "*Get out!*"

He looked up in shock and whirled about. His eyes widened in astonishment. The command had come from directly behind him, but he was alone in the room. Who or whatever had spoken, was nowhere to be seen!

When he finished his ritual of blessing, the priest didn't mention the incident to the Lutzes. They thanked him for his kindness, asked him to stay for supper, such as it would be the first night. He politely refused, explaining that he planned to have dinner with his mother at her house in Nassau. She would be waiting for him; it was getting late, and he still had a bit of a drive.

Kathy really wanted to thank Father Mancuso for his contribution to the occasion. George asked if he would accept a gift of money or a bottle of Canadian Club, but he quickly refused, stating he couldn't accept gratuities from a friend.

Once in his car, Father Mancuso rolled down his window. Repeated thanks and well-wishes were exchanged, but as he spoke to the couple, his expression turned serious. "By the way, George. I had lunch with some friends over in Lindenhurst before coming here. They told me that this was the DeFeo home. Did you know that?"

"Oh, sure. I think that's why it's such a bargain. It was on the market for a long time. But that doesn't bother us at all. It's got the best of everything."

"Wasn't that a tragedy, Father?" said Kathy. "That poor family. Imagine, all six murdered in their sleep."

The priest nodded. Then with repeated goodbyes from the three children, the family watched as he drove off to Queens.

It was nearly four when George had completed the first unloading at 112 Ocean Avenue. He drove the U-Haul back to Deer Park and into his old driveway. As he opened the door to his garage, Harry, his dog, leaped out and would have made a getaway if he hadn't been snared by his head. The fast and sturdy half-malamute, half-Labrador retriever had been left behind to guard the rest of the family's belongings. Now George took him into the truck with him.

As Father Mancuso rode toward his mother's, he tried to rationalize what had happened to him in the Lutzes' house. Who or what would say such a thing to him. After all his experiences in counseling, now and again in his sessions he encountered clients who reported hearing voices—a symptom of psychosis. But Father Mancuso was convinced of his own stability.

His mother greeted him at her door, then frowned. "What's the matter with you, Frank? Don't you feel well?"

The priest shook his head. "No, not too terribly."

"Go in the bathroom and look at your face."

Looking at his reflection in the mirror, he saw two large, black circles under his eyes that were so dark he thought they must be smears of dirt. He tried to wash them off with soap and water, but it didn't help.

Back in Amityville, George took Harry to the dog compound next to the garage and chained him with a 20-foot steel lead. Now that it was after six, George was almost exhausted and decided to leave the rest of his possessions in the truck even though it was costing him fifty dollars a day to rent the vehicle. He worked inside, placing most of the living room furniture in their approximate positions.

Father Mancuso left his mother's home after eight, heading back to the Rectory. On the Van Wyck Expressway in Queens, he found his car was literally being forced onto the right shoulder. He looked around quickly. There was no other vehicle within fifty feet of him!

Shortly after driving back onto the highway and continuing on his way, the hood suddenly flew open, smashing back against the windshield. One of the welded hinges tore loose. The right door flew open! Frantically Father Mancuso tried to brake the car. Then it stalled by itself.

Shaken, he finally got to a telephone and reached another priest who lived near the Expressway. Fortunately the other cleric was able to drive Father Mancuso to a garage where he hired a tow truck to bring in the disabled car. Back on the Expressway, the mechanic could not get the Ford to start. Father Mancuso decided to leave the vehicle at the garage and have his friend drive him on to the Sacred Heart Rectory.

Coming to almost the very end of his strength, George decided to complete the day's labor with something more pleasurable for himself. He'd rig his stereo up with the hi-fi equipment that the DeFeos had built into the living room. Then he and Kathy would have music to add to the joy of their first night in their new home.

He'd barely begun the job, when Harry began an awful howling outside. Danny came rushing into the house, yelling that Harry was in trouble. George ran out to the back fence to find the poor animal strangling. He had tried to jump over the fence and was now choking on his chain, which had looped across the top bar. George freed Harry, shortened the lead so the dog couldn't try that again, and returned to installing the stereo.

* * *

An hour after he was back in his quarters, Father Mancuso's telephone rang. It was the priest who had helped him out earlier. "Do you know what happened to me after I dropped you off?"

Father Mancuso was almost afraid to ask . . .

"The windshield wipers, they began to fly back and forth like crazy! I couldn't stop them! I never turned them on, Frank! What the hell is going on?"

By eleven o'clock that night, the Lutzes were ready to settle down for their first night in their new home. It had gotten colder outside, down to almost 6 degrees above zero. George burned some now-empty cardboard cartons in the fireplace, making a merry blaze. It was the eighteenth of December, 1975, the first of their twenty-eight days.

3 **December 19 to 21** — George sat up in bed, wide awake. He had heard a knock on his front door.

He looked around in the darkness. For a moment, he didn't know where he was, but then it came to him. He was in the master bedroom of his new home. Kathy was there, beside him, hunched down under the warm covers.

The knock came again. "Jesus, who's that?" he muttered.

George reached for his wristwatch on the night table. It was 3:15 in the morning! Again a loud rapping. Only this time, it didn't sound as if it was coming from downstairs, more from somewhere off to his left.

George got out of bed, padded across the cold, un-carpeted floor of the hallway and into the sewing room that faced the Amityville River in the back. He looked out the window into the darkness. He heard another knock. George strained his eyes to see. "Where the hell's Harry?"

From somewhere over his head came a sharp crack. Instinctively he ducked, then looked up at the ceiling. He heard a low squeak. The boys, Danny and Chris, were on the floor above him. One of them must have pushed a toy off his bed in his sleep.

Barefooted and wearing only his pajama pants, George was shivering now. He looked back out the window. There! Something *was* moving, down by the boathouse. He quickly lifted the window, and the freez-ing air hit him full blast. "Hey! Who's out there?" Then Harry barked and moved. George, his eyes adjusting to the darkness, saw the dog spring to his feet. The shadow was close to Harry.

"Harry! Go get him!" Another rap sounded from the direction of the boathouse, and Harry spun around at the noise. He began running back and forth in his com-pound, barking furiously now, the lead holding him back.

George slammed the window shut and ran back to his bedroom. Kathy had awoken. "What's the matter?" She turned on the lamp on her night table as George fumbled into his pants. "George?" Kathy saw his bearded face look up.

"It's all right, honey. I just want to take a look around out back. Harry's onto something near the boat-house. Probably a cat. I'd better quiet him down before he wakes the whole neighborhood." He slid into his loafers and was heading for his old navy blue Marine parka lying on a chair. "I'll be right up. Go back to sleep."

Kathy turned off the light. "Okay. Put your jacket on." The next morning, she wouldn't remember having awakened at all.

When George came out the kitchen door, Harry was still barking at the moving shadow. There was a length of two-by-four lumber lying against the swimming pool fence. George grabbed it and ran toward the boathouse. Then he saw the shadow move. His grip tightened on the heavy stick. Another loud rap.

"Damn!" George saw it was the door to the boathouse, open and swinging in the wind. "I thought I'd locked that before!"

Harry barked again.

"Oh, shut up, Harry! Knock it off!"

A half hour later, George was back in bed, still wide awake. As an ex-Marine, not too many years out of the service, he was fairly accustomed to emergency wake-up calls. It was taking him time to turn off his inner alarm system.

Waiting for sleep to return, he considered what he had gotten himself into—a second marriage with three children, a new house with a big mortgage. The taxes in Amityville were three times higher than in Deer Park. Did he really need that new speedboat? How the hell was he going to pay for all of this? The construction business was lousy on Long Island because of the tight mortgage money, and it didn't look like it would get better until the banks loosened up. If they aren't building houses and buying property, who the hell needs a land surveyor?

Kathy shifted in her sleep, so that her arm fell across George's neck. Her face burrowed deep into his chest.

He sniffed her hair. She certainly smelled clean, he thought; he liked that. And she kept her children the same way, spotless. *Her* kids? George's now. Whatever the trouble, she and the children were worth it.

George looked up at the ceiling. Danny was a good boy, into everything. He could handle almost anything you gave him to do. They were getting closer, now. Danny was now beginning to call his stepfather "Dad"; no more "George." In a way he was glad he never got to meet Kathy's ex-husband; this way he felt Danny was all his. Kathy said that Chris looked just like his father, had the same ways about him, the same dark, curly hair and eyes. George would reprimand the boy for something, and Chris's face would fall and he'd look up at him with those soulful eyes. The kid sure knew how to use them.

He liked the way both boys looked after little Missy. She was a little terror, but smart for a five year old. He'd never had any trouble with her from the first day he met Kathy. She was Daddy's girl, all right. Listens to Kathy and me. In fact, they all do. They're three nice kids I've got.

It was after six before George finally fell into a deep sleep. Kathy woke up a few minutes later.

She looked around this strange room, trying to put her thoughts together. She was in the bedroom of her beautiful new home. Her husband was next to her and her three children were in their own bedrooms. Wasn't that marvelous! God had been good to them.

Kathy tried to slip easily from under George's arm. The poor man worked so hard yesterday, she thought, and today he's got more ahead of him. Let him sleep. She couldn't; she had too much to do in the kitchen and she had better get started before the kids got up.

Downstairs, she looked around at her new kitchen. It was still dark outside. She turned on the light. Boxes of her dishes, glasses, and pots were piled up all over the floor and sink. Chairs were still sitting on top of the dinette table. But, she smiled to herself, the kitchen was going to be a happy room for her family. It might be just the place for her Transcendental Meditation, which George had been practicing for two years; Kathy, one. He had been into TM ever since the breakup of his first marriage, when he had been attending sessions of group therapy; out of that grew his interest in meditation. He had introduced Kathy to the subject, but now, with all the work of moving in, he had completely ignored his established pattern of going off by himself into a room and meditating for a few minutes each day.

Kathy washed out her electric percolator, filled it, plugged it in, and lit her first cigarette of the day. Drinking coffee, Kathy sat at the table with a pad and pencil, making notes for herself on the jobs to be done around the house. Today was the nineteenth, a Friday. The kids would not go to their new school until after the Christmas holidays. Christmas! There was so much still to do. . . .

Kathy sensed someone was staring at her. Startled, she looked up and over her shoulder. Her little daughter was standing in the doorway. "Missy! You scared me half to death. What's the matter? What are you doing up so early?"

The little girl's eyes were half-closed. Her blonde hair hung across her face. She looked around, as if not understanding where she was. "I wanna go home, Mama."

"You *are* home, Missy. This is our new home. C'mere."

Missy shambled over to Kathy and climbed up on her mother's lap. The two ladies of the house sat there in their pleasant kitchen, Kathy rocking her daughter back to sleep.

George came down after nine. By that time, the boys had already finished their breakfast and were outside, playing with Harry, investigating everything. Missy was asleep again in her room.

Kathy looked at her husband whose big frame filled the doorway. She saw he hadn't shaved below his jawbone and that his dark blonde hair and beard were still uncombed. That meant he hadn't showered. "What's the matter? Aren't you going to work?"

George sat down wearily at the table. "Nope. I still have to unload the truck and get it back out to Deer Park. We blew an extra fifty bucks by keeping it overnight." He looked around, yawning, and shivered. "It's cold in here. Don't you have the heat on?"

The boys ran past the kitchen door, yelling at Harry. George looked up. "What's the matter with those two? Can't you keep them quiet, Kathy?"

She turned from the sink. "Well, don't bark at me! *You're* their father, you know! You do it!"

George slapped his open palm down on the table. The sharp sound made Kathy jump. "Right!" he shouted.

George opened the kitchen door and leaned out. Danny, Chris, and Harry, whooping it up, ran by again. "Okay! The three of you! Knock it off!" Without waiting for their reactions, he slammed the door and stormed out of the kitchen.

Kathy was speechless. This was the first time he had really lost his temper with the children. And for so little! He hadn't been in a bad mood the day before.

George unloaded the U-Haul by himself, then drove it back to Deer Park, with his motorcycle in the rear so that he could get back to Amityville. He never did shave or shower and did nothing the rest of the day but gripe about the lack of heat in the house and the noise the children were making in their playroom up on the third floor.

He had been a bear all day, and by eleven o'clock that night, when it was time to go to bed, Kathy was ready to crown him. She was exhausted from putting things away and trying to keep the kids away from George. She'd start cleaning the bathrooms in the morning, she figured, but that was it for tonight. *She* was going to bed.

George stayed down in the living room, feeding log after log into the roaring fireplace. Even though the thermostat read 75 degrees, he couldn't seem to get warm. He must have checked the oil burner in the basement a dozen times during the day and evening.

At twelve, George finally dragged himself up to the bedroom and fell asleep immediately. At 3:15 in the morning, he was wide awake again, sitting up in bed.

There was something on his mind. The boathouse. Did he lock the door? He couldn't remember. He had to go out and check. It was closed and locked up.

Over the next two days, the Lutz family began to go through a collective personality change. As George said, "It was not a big thing, just little bits and pieces, here and there." He didn't shave or shower, something he did religiously. Normally George devoted as much time to his business as he could; two years before, he had had a second office in Shirley to handle contractors farther out on the South Shore. But now he simply called Syosset and gave gruff orders to his men, demanding they finish some surveying jobs over the weekend because he needed the money. As for arranging to move his office to his new basement setup, he never gave it another thought.

Instead, George constantly complained the house was like a refrigerator and he had to warm it up. Stuffing more and more logs in the fireplace occupied almost his every moment, except for the times he would go out to the boathouse, stare into space, then go back to the house. Even now, he can't say what he was looking for when he went there; he just knew that somehow he was drawn to the place.

It was practically a compulsion. The third night in the house, he again awoke at 3:15 A.M., worried about what might be going on out there.

The children bothered him too. Ever since the move, they seemed to have become brats, misbehaved monsters who wouldn't listen, unruly children who must be severely punished.

When it came to the children, Kathy fell into the same mood. She was tense from her strained relationship with George and from the efforts of trying to put her house in shape before Christmas. On their fourth night in the house, she exploded and together with her husband, beat Danny, Chris, and Missy with a strap and a large, heavy wooden spoon.

The children had accidentally cracked a pane of glass in the playroom's half-moon window.

4 **December 22** — Early Monday morning, it was bitter cold in Amityville. The town is right on the Atlantic side of Long Island and the sea wind blew in like a nor'easter. The thermometer hovered at 8 degrees and media weathermen were forecasting a white Christmas.

Inside 112 Ocean Avenue, Danny, Chris, and Missy Lutz were up in the playroom, slightly subdued from the whipping the night before. George had still not gone to his office and was sitting in the living room, adding more logs to a blazing fire. Kathy was writing at her dinette table in the kitchen nook.

As she worked over a list of things to buy for Christmas, her concentration wandered. She was upset about having hit the children, particularly about the way George and she had gone about it. There were many gifts the Lutz family still hadn't bought, and Kathy knew she had to go out and get them, but since they had moved in, she never had any desire to leave the house. She had just written down her Aunt Theresa's name when Kathy froze, pencil in midair.

Something had come up from behind and embraced her. Then it took her hand and gave it a pat. The touch was reassuring, and had an inner strength to it. Kathy was startled, but not frightened; it was like the touch of a mother giving comfort to her daughter. Kathy had the impression of a woman's soft hand resting on her own!

"Mommy! Come up here, quick!" It was Chris, calling from the third floor hallway.

Kathy looked up. The spell was broken, the touch was gone. She ran up the stairs to her children. They were in their bathroom, looking into the toilet. Kathy saw the inside of the bowl was absolutely black, as though someone had painted it from the bottom to the edge just below the rim. She pushed the handle, flushing clear water against the sides. The black remained.

Kathy grabbed toilet paper and tried vainly to rub off the discoloration. "I don't believe it! I just scrubbed this yesterday with Clorox!" She turned accusingly to the children. "Did you throw any paint in here?"

"Oh, no Mama!" all three chorused.

Kathy was fit to be tied; the incident in the breakfast nook was forgotten. She looked into the sink and bathtub, but they were still gleaming from her scouring. She turned on the faucets. Nothing but clear running water.

Once more, she flushed the toilet, not really expecting the horrible black color to disappear.

She bent down and looked around the base to see if anything was leaking through to the inside of the bowl. Finally she turned to Danny. "Get the Clorox from my bathroom. It's in the little closet under the sink."

Missy started to go. "Missy! You stay here! Let Danny get it." The boy left the bathroom. "And bring the scrub brush, too!" Kathy called after him.

Chris searched his mother's face, his eyes watering. "I didn't do it. Please don't hit me again."

Kathy looked at him, thinking of the terrible night before. "No, baby, it wasn't your fault. Something's happened to the water, I think. Maybe some oil backed up the line. Didn't you notice it before?"

"I had to go. I saw it first!" crowed Missy.

"Uh-huh. Well, let's see what the Clorox does before I call your father and he. . . ."

"Mama! Mama!" The cry came from down the hall.

Kathy leaned out the bathroom doorway. "What is it, Danny? I said it's under the sink!"

"No, Mama! I found it! But the black's in your toilet, too! And it stinks in here!"

Kathy's bathroom door was at the far end of her bedroom. Danny was standing outside the bedroom, holding his nose, when Kathy and the other two children came running down.

As soon as Kathy stepped into the bedroom, the odor hit her—a sweetish perfume smell. She stopped, sniffed, and frowned. "What the hell is *that*? That isn't my cologne."

But when she entered her bathroom, she was struck by a completely different odor, an overpowering stench. Kathy gagged and started to cough, but before she ran, caught a glimpse of her toilet bowl. It was totally black inside!

The children scrambled out of her way as she headed down the stairs. "George!"

"What do you want? I'm busy!"

Kathy burst into the living room and ran over to where George was crouched by the fireplace. "You'd better come and look! There's something in our bathroom that smells like a dead rat! And the toilet's all black!" She grabbed his hand and tugged him out of the room.

The other bathroom toilet bowl on the second floor was also black inside, as George discovered, but it had no smell. He sniffed the perfume in his room. "What the hell's that?"

He began to open the windows on the second floor. "First, let's get this smell out of here!" He lifted the windows in his and Kathy's bedroom, then ran across the hall to the other bedrooms. Then he heard Kathy's voice.

"George! Look at this!"

The fourth bedroom on the second floor—now Kathy's sewing room—has two windows. One, which looks out at the boathouse and the Amityville River, was the window George had opened that first night when he had awakened at 3:15. The other faces the neighboring house to the right of 112 Ocean Avenue. On this window, clinging to the inside of the panes, were literally hundreds of buzzing flies!

"Jesus, will you look at that! House flies, *now*?"

"Maybe they're attracted by the smell?" Kathy volunteered.

"Yeah, but not at this time of year. Flies don't live

that long, and not in this weather. And why are they only on this window?" George looked around the room, trying to see where the insects had come from. There was a closet in one corner. He opened the door and peered in, looking for cracks; for anything that would make sense.

"If this closet wall was up against the bathroom, they might have lived in the warmth. But this wall's against the outside." George put his hand against the plaster. "It's cold in here. I don't see any way they could have survived."

After shooing his family out into the hall, George shut the door to the sewing room. He opened the other window overlooking the boathouse, then took some newspapers and chased out as many flies as he could. He killed those that remained, then he closed the window. By then, it was freezing on the second floor, but at least the sweet perfume odor was gone. The bathroom stench had also diminished.

This didn't help George in his efforts to warm his house. Though no one else was complaining, he checked the oil heating system in the basement. It was working fine. By four o'clock in the afternoon, the thermostat just off the living room read 80 degrees, but George couldn't feel the heat.

Kathy had scrubbed the toilet bowls again with Clorox, Fantastik, and Lysol. The cleaners helped somewhat, but a good deal of the black remained, stained deep into the porcelain. Worst of all was the toilet in the second bathroom next to the sewing room.

The outdoor temperature had risen to 20 degrees and the children were out of the house, playing with Harry. Kathy warned them to keep away from the boathouse and bulkhead area, saying it was too dangerous for them to play there without someone to watch them.

George had brought in some more logs from the cord stacked in the garage and was sitting in the kitchen with Kathy. They began to argue violently about who should go out to buy the Christmas gifts. "Why can't you at least pick up the perfume for your mother?" asked George.

"I've got to get this place in order," Kathy erupted. "I don't see you doing anything but harping!"

After a few minutes, the squabble petered out. Kathy was about to mention the eerie thing that had happened to her in the nook that morning when the front doorbell rang.

A man, who looked to be anywhere from thirty-five to forty-five because of his receding hairline, was standing there with a hesitant smile on his face and a six-pack of beer in his hands. His features were coarse and his nose was red from the cold. "Everybody wants to come over to welcome you to the neighborhood. You don't mind, do you?"

The fellow wore a three-quarter length wool car coat, corduroy pants, and construction boots. It struck George that he didn't look like a neighbor who would own one of the large homes in the area.

Before they even moved to Amityville, George and Kathy had considered the idea of having an open house, but once in the new house, they had never brought up the subject again. George nodded to the one-man welcoming committee. "No, we don't mind. If they don't mind sitting on cardboard boxes, bring them all."

George took him into the kitchen and introduced

Kathy. The man stood there, and repeated his speech to her. Kathy nodded. He continued by telling the Lutzes that he kept his boat at another neighbor's boathouse, several doors down on Ocean Avenue.

The man held on to the six-pack and finally said, "I brought it, I'll take it with me," and left.

George and Kathy never found out his name. They never saw him again.

That night when they went to bed, George made his usual check of all the doors and windows, latching and locking, inside and out. So, when he woke once more at 3:15 in the morning and gave in to the urge to look downstairs, he was stunned to find the two hundred and fifty pound wooden front door wrenched wide open, hanging from one hinge!

5 December 23 — Kathy awoke to the noise of George wrestling with the wrecked front door. When she felt the chill in the house, she threw on a robe and ran downstairs to see her husband trying to force the heavy wooden slab back into its frame.

"What happened?"

"I don't *know*," George answered, finally forcing the door closed. "This thing was wide open, hanging on one hinge. Here, look at this!" He pointed to the brass lock plate. The doorknob was twisted completely off-center. The metal facing was bent back as though someone had tried to pry it open with a tool, but from

43

the *inside*! "Someone was trying to get *out* of the house, not in!"

"I don't understand what's going on around here," George muttered, more to himself than Kathy. "I know I locked this before I went upstairs. To open the door from in here, all you had to do was turn the lock."

"Is it the same way outside?" Kathy asked.

"No. There's nothing wrong with the knob or the outside plate. Somebody'd need an awful lot of strength to pull away a door this heavy and tear it off one of the hinges. . . ."

"Maybe it was the wind, George," Kathy offered hopefully. "It seems to get pretty strong out there, you know."

"There's no wind in *here*, much less a tornado. Somebody or something had to do this!"

The Lutzes looked at one another. Kathy was the first to react. "The kids!" She turned and ran up the stairs to the second floor and into Missy's bedroom.

A small light in the shape of Yogi Bear was plugged into the wall near the bottom of the little girl's bed. In its feeble glow, Kathy glimpsed the form of Missy lying on her stomach. "Missy?" Kathy whispered, leaning over the bed. Missy whimpered, then turned over onto her back.

Kathy let out a sigh of relief and tucked the covers up under her daughter's chin. The cold air that had come in while the front door was open had made even this room very chilly. She kissed Missy on the forehead and silently slipped out of the room, heading for the third floor.

Danny and Chris were sleeping soundly. Both were on their stomachs. "Later, when I thought about it," Kathy says, "that was the first time I could ever remember the children sleeping in that position—particularly all three on their stomachs at the same time. I even remember I was almost going to say something to George, that it was kind of strange."

In the morning, the cold spell that gripped Amityville was still unbroken. It was cloudy, and the radio kept promising snow for Christmas. In the hallway of the Lutz home, the thermostat still read a steady 80 degrees, but George was back in the living room, stoking the fire to a roaring blaze. He told Kathy he just couldn't shake the chill from his bones, and he didn't understand why she and the children didn't feel that way too.

The job of replacing the doorknob and lock assembly on the front door was too complex for even a handy individual like George. The local locksmith arrived about twelve, as he'd promised. He made a long, slow survey of the damage inside the house and then gave George a peculiar look, but offered no explanation as to how something like this could have possibly happened.

He finished the job quickly and quietly. Upon leaving, his one comment was that the DeFeos had called him a couple of years before: "They were having trouble with the lock on the boathouse door." He had been called to change the lock assembly because once the door was closed from the inside, it would somehow jam, and whoever was in the boathouse couldn't get out.

George wanted to say more about the boathouse, but when Kathy looked at him, he held back. They didn't want the news spreading around Amityville that again there was something funny going on at 112 Ocean Avenue.

45

By two in the afternoon, the weather had begun to warm. A slight drizzle was enough to keep the children in the house. George still hadn't gone to work and was in constant transit between the living room and the basement, adding logs and checking on the oil burner. Danny and Chris were up in their third floor playroom, noisily banging their toys around. Kathy was back at her cleaning chores, putting shelf paper in the closets. She had worked her way almost to her own bedroom on the second floor when she looked in Missy's room. The little girl was sitting in her diminutive rocking chair, humming to herself as she stared out the window that looked toward the boathouse.

Kathy was about to speak to her daughter when the phone rang. She picked up the extension in her own bedroom. It was her mother, saying that she would be over the next day—Christmas Eve—and that Kathy's brother Jimmy would bring them a Christmas tree as a housewarming gift.

Kathy said how relieved she was that at least the tree would be taken care of, since she and George had been unable to rouse themselves to do any shopping at all. Then, out of the corner of her eye, Kathy saw Missy leave her room and enter the sewing room. Kathy was only half listening to what her mother was saying; what could Missy possibly want in there, where all the flies had been the day before? She could hear her five-year-old daughter humming, moving about some still-unopened cardboard boxes.

Kathy was about to cut her mother short when she saw Missy come back out of the sewing room. When the child stepped into the hallway and returned to her own bedroom, she stopped her humming. Puzzled by her daughter's behavior, Kathy wound up her conversation with her mother, again thanking her for the tree. She hung up, walked silently toward Missy's room and stood in the doorway.

Missy was back in her rocking chair, staring out the same window and humming again, a tune that didn't sound quite familiar. Kathy was about to speak when Missy stopped humming, and without turning her head, said, "Mama? Do angels talk?"

Kathy stared at her daughter. The little girl had known she was there! But before Kathy could step into the room, she was startled by a loud crash from overhead. The boys were upstairs! Fearful, she raced up the steps to the playroom. Danny and Chris were rolling on the floor, locked in each other's arms, punching and kicking at each other.

"What's going on here?" Kathy screamed. "Danny! Chris! You stop this right now, you hear!" She tried to pull them apart, but each was still trying to get at the other, their eyes blazing with hate. Chris was crying in his anger. It was the first time, *ever*, that the two brothers had gotten into a fight.

She slapped each boy in the face—hard—and demanded to know what had started this nonsense. "Danny started it," Chris sniffed.

"Liar! Chris, *you* started it," Danny scowled.

"Started *what*? What are you fighting about?" Kathy demanded, her voice rising. There was no answer from either boy. Both suddenly withdrew from their mother. Whatever happened, Kathy sensed it was their affair not hers.

Then her patience snapped. "What is going on around here? First it's Missy with her angels, and now you two idiots trying to kill each other! Well, I've had it! We'll just see what your father has to say about all

47

this. You're both going to get it later, but right now I don't want to hear another peep out of either of you! You hear me? Not another sound!"

Shaking, Kathy returned downstairs to her shelving. *Cool down*, she told herself. As she passed Missy's room again, the little girl was humming the same strange tune to herself. Kathy wanted to go in, but then thought better of it and continued on into her own bedroom. She'd talk to George later when she had a chance to be calmer about the whole affair.

Kathy picked up a roll of shelf paper and opened the door to the walk-in closet. Immediately a sour smell struck her nostrils. "Oh, God! What's that?" She pulled the light chain hanging from the closet ceiling and looked around the small room. It was empty except for one thing. On the very first day the Lutzes had moved in, she had hung a crucifix on the inner wall facing the closet door, just as she had done when they lived in Deer Park. A friend had originally given her the crucifix as a wedding present. Made of silver, it was a beautiful piece about twelve inches long and had been blessed a long time before.

As Kathy looked at it now, her eyes widened in horror. She began to gag at the sour smell, but couldn't retreat from the sight of the crucifix—now hanging upside down!

6 December 24 — It was almost a week since Father Mancuso had visited 112 Ocean Avenue. The eerie episodes of that day and night were still very much on his mind, but he had discussed them with no one—not with George and Kathy Lutz, not even with his Confessor.

During the night of the twenty-third, he had come down with the flu. The priest had alternated between chills and sweating, and when he finally got up to take his temperature, the thermometer read 103 degrees. He took some aspirin, hoping to break the fever. This was the Christmas season, and with it began a host of clerical duties—a particularly bad time for a priest to be indisposed.

Father Mancuso fell into a troubled sleep. Around four in the morning of Christmas Eve, he awoke to find his temperature now up to 104 degrees. He called the Pastor to his rooms. His friend decided to get a doctor. While Father Mancuso waited for the physician, he thought again of the Lutz family.

There was something he couldn't quite put his finger on. He kept envisioning a room he believed to be on the second floor of the house. His head swam, but the priest could see it clearly in his mind. It was filled with unopened boxes when he had blessed the home, and he remembered he could see the boathouse from its windows.

Father Mancuso recalls that while ill in bed, he used the word "evil" to himself, but thinks the high fever might have been playing tricks with his imagination. He also remembers he had an urge, bordering on obsession, to call the Lutzes and warn them to stay out of that room at all costs.

At the same time, in Amityville, Kathy Lutz was also thinking about the room on the second floor. Every once in a while, Kathy felt the need for some time to be by herself, and this was to be her own personal room. She had also considered the room, along with the kitchen, for her meditation. That third bedroom on the second floor would also serve as a dressing room and storage place for her and George's growing wardrobes.

Among the cartons in the sewing room were boxes of Christmas ornaments that she had accumulated over the years. It was time to unwrap the balls and lights, get them ready to put on the tree her mother and brother had promised to bring over that evening.

After lunch, Kathy asked Danny and Chris to bring the cartons down to the living room. George was more interested in his fireplace logs and only halfheartedly worked on the Christmas lights, testing the many colored bulbs and disentangling their wires. For the next few hours, Kathy and the children were busy unwrapping tissue paper that enclosed the delicate, bright-colored balls; the little wooden and glass angels, Santas, skaters, ballerinas, reindeer and snowmen that Kathy had added to each year as the children grew up.

Each child had his own favorite ornaments and tenderly placed them on towels Kathy had spread on the floor. Some dated back to Danny's first Christmas. But today, the children were admiring an ornament that George had brought to his new family. It was an heirloom, a unique galaxy of crescents and stars wrought in sterling silver and encased in 24 karat gold. There was a fixture on the back of the 6-inch ornament that let one attach it to a tree. Crafted in Germany more than a century before, it had been given to George by his grandmother, who in turn had received it from her own grandmother.

The doctor had come and gone from the Rectory. He confirmed that Father Mancuso did indeed have the flu and advised the ailing priest to remain in bed for a day or so. The fever was in his system and could remain high for another twenty-four hours.

Father Mancuso chafed at the idea of remaining idle. He had so much work to do. He agreed that upcoming items on his busy calendar could be put off for a week, but some of his clients in counseling could not afford the same kind of postponement. Nevertheless, both the physician and the Pastor insisted that Father Mancuso would only prolong his illness if he insisted upon working or leaving his apartment.

There was one thing he could still do, however, and that was to call George Lutz. The bad feeling he had about the second-floor room remained and it made him as restless as his fever. When he finally made the call, it was five P.M.

Danny answered the telephone and ran to get his father. Kathy was surprised by the call, but not George. Sitting by the fireplace, he had been thinking about the priest all day. George had felt an urge to call Father Mancuso, but couldn't decide just what he wanted to say.

He was sorry to hear of Father Mancuso's flu and asked if there was anything he could do. Assured there was nothing any man could do to relieve the priest's discomfort, George began to speak of what was happening at the house. At first it was a light conversation; George told Father Mancuso about bringing down the ornaments to trim the Christmas tree that Jimmy, his brother-in-law, would be delivering at any moment.

Father Mancuso interrupted George. "I have to talk to you about something that's been on my mind. Do you know the room on your second floor that faces the boathouse—the one where you had all those unopened boxes and cartons?"

"Sure, Father. That's going to be Kathy's sewing and meditation room when I get a chance to fix it up. Hey, you know what we found in there the other day? Flies! Hundreds of houseflies! Can you imagine, in the middle of winter!"

George waited for the priest's reaction. He got it.

"George, I don't want you, or Kathy, or the children to go back into that room. You have to stay out of there!"

"Why, Father? What's up there?"

Before the priest could answer, there was a loud crackling sound on the telephone. Both men pulled back from their earpieces in surprise. George couldn't make out Father Mancuso's next words. All that remained was an irritating static noise. "Hello! Hello! Father? I can't hear you! There must be a bad connection!"

From his end, Father Mancuso was also trying to hear George through the static and only faintly heard the "Hello's." Finally the priest hung up, then dialed the Lutzes' number again. He could hear the phone ringing, but no one picked it up. The priest waited for ten rings before finally giving up. He was very disturbed.

When he could no longer hear Father Mancuso through the crackling, George had also hung up his receiver. He waited for the priest to call back. For several minutes he sat in the kitchen and stared at the silent telephone. Then he dialed Father Mancuso's private number at the Rectory.

There was no answer.

In the living room, Kathy began wrapping the few Christmas gifts she had accumulated before moving to Amityville. She had gone to sales at Sears and to the Green Acres Shopping Center in Valley Stream, picking up bargains in clothing for her children and other items for George and her family. Sadly, Kathy noted that the pile of boxes was rather small and silently berated herself for not leaving the house to go out shopping. There were few toys for Danny, Chris, and Missy, but it was too late to do anything about it.

She had sent the children up to the playroom so she could work alone. She thought about Missy. She had not answered her daughter's question about talking angels—Kathy had put it off by telling Missy she'd ask Daddy about it. But it never came up when she and George went to bed. Why would Missy come up with such an idea? Did it have anything to do with the child's peculiar behavior yesterday in her bedroom? And what was she looking for in the sewing room?

Kathy's concentration was broken when George returned from the phone in the kitchen. He had an odd expression on his face and was avoiding her gaze. Kathy waited for him to tell her about Father Mancuso when the front doorbell rang. She looked around, startled. "It must be my mother! George, they're here already and I haven't even started supper!" She hurried toward the kitchen. "You get the door!"

Kathy's brother, Jimmy Conners, was a big, strapping youth who genuinely liked George. That evening, his face exuded a special warmth and charm. He was to be married on the day after Christmas and had asked George to be his best man. But when mother and son entered the house, Jimmy lugging a sizable Scotch pine, both their faces changed at the sight of George, who hadn't shaved or showered for almost a week. Kathy's mother, Joan, was alarmed. "Where are Kathy and the kids?" she asked George.

"She's making supper, and they're up in the playroom. Why?"

"I just had the feeling something was wrong."

This was the first time his in-laws had visited the house, so George had to show his mother-in-law where the kitchen was located. Then he and Jimmy hefted the tree into the living room. "Boy! That's some fire you've got going there!"

George explained that he just couldn't warm up; hadn't been able to since the day they moved in, and that he had already burned ten logs that day. "Yeah," Jimmy agreed. "It does seem kind of chilly around here. Maybe there's something wrong with your burner or thermostat?"

"No," answered George. "The oil burner's working fine and the thermostat's up to 80 degrees. Come on down to the basement and I'll show you."

In the Rectory, Father Mancuso's doctor had warned him that one's body temperature normally rises after five in the afternoon. Even though he was uncomfortable and his stomach hurt, the priest's mind kept turning to the strange telephone problems the Lutzes were having.

It was now eight o'clock, and his repeated attempts to contact George had been fruitless. Several times he had asked the operator to check to see if the Lutzes' phone was out of order. Each time it rang interminably until a supervisor called him back to report no service problems with the line.

Why hadn't George called him back? Father Mancuso was sure George had heard what he said about the second floor room. Was there now something terribly wrong? Father Mancuso did not trust 112 Ocean Avenue, he could wait no longer. He dialed a number he normally used only for emergencies.

The Christmas tree was up at the Lutzes' home. Danny, Chris, and Missy were helping their Uncle

55

Jimmy trim it, each urging him to hang his *own* ornaments first. George had returned to his own private world by the fireplace. Kathy and her mother were in the kitchen talking. This was her "happy" room, the one place in the new house where she felt secure.

She complained to her mother that George had changed since they moved in. "Ma, he won't take a shower, he won't shave. He doesn't even leave the house to go to the office. All he does is sit by that damned fireplace and complain about the cold. And another thing—every night he keeps going out to check that boathouse."

"What's he looking for?" Mrs. Conners asked.

"Who knows? All he keeps saying is he's got to look around out there—and check on the boat."

"That's doesn't sound like George. Have you asked him if there's anything the matter?"

"Oh, sure!" Kathy threw up her hands. "And all he does is throw more wood on the fire! In one week, we've gone through almost a whole cord of wood."

Kathy's mother shivered and pulled her sweater tighter around her body. "Well, you know, it *is* kind of chilly in the house. I've felt it ever since I came in."

Jimmy, standing on a chair in the living room, was about to fix George's ornament to the top of the tree. He too shivered. "Hey, George, you got a door opened someplace? I keep getting a draft on the back of my neck."

George looked up. "No, I don't think so. I locked up everything before." He felt a sudden urge to check the second floor sewing room. "I'll be right back."

Kathy and Mrs. Conners passed him as they came in from the kitchen. He didn't say a word to either woman, just ran up the stairs. "What's with him?" Mrs. Conners asked.

Kathy just shrugged. "See what I mean?" She began to arrange the Christmas gifts under the tree. When Danny, Chris, and Missy counted the meager number of prettily wrapped packages on the floor, there was a chorus of disappointed voices behind her.

"What are you crying about?" George was back, standing in the doorway. "Knock it off! You kids are too spoiled anyway!"

Kathy was about to snap back at her husband for yelling at the children in front of her mother and brother when she saw the look on George's face.

"Did you open the window in the sewing room, Kathy?"

"Me? I haven't been up there all day."

George turned to the children near the tree. "Have any of you kids been in that room since you brought down the Christmas boxes?" All three shook their heads. George hadn't moved from his position in the doorway. His eyes returned to Kathy.

"George, what is it?"

"A window is open. And the flies are back."

Crack! Everyone in the room jumped at the loud sound that came from somewhere outside. Again came a sharp knock, and outside, Harry barked. "The boathouse door! It's open again!" George turned to Jimmy. "Don't leave them alone! I'll be right back!" He grabbed his parka from the hall closet and headed for the kitchen door. Kathy began to cry.

"Kathy, what's going on?" Mrs. Conners said, her voice rising.

"Oh, Mama! I don't know!"

* * *

A man watched as George came out of a side door and ran toward the back of the house. He knew the door led from the kitchen because he had been at 112 Ocean Avenue before. He sat in a car parked in front of the Lutzes' home and observed George shut the boathouse door.

He glanced at his watch. It was almost eleven o'clock. The man picked up the microphone of a car radio. "Zammataro. This is Gionfriddo. You can call your friend back and tell him the people in 112 Ocean Avenue are home." Sergeant Al Gionfriddo of the Suffolk County Police Department was doing a job this Christmas Eve, just as he had been on the night of the DeFeo family massacre.

7 **December 25** — For the seventh night in a row, George awoke at exactly 3:15. He sat up in bed. In the winter moonlight flooding the bedroom, George saw Kathy quite clearly. She was sleeping on her stomach.

He reached out his hand to touch her head. At that instant, Kathy woke up. As she looked wildly about, George could see the fright in her eyes. "She was shot in the head!" Kathy yelled. "She was shot in the head! I heard the explosions in my head!"

Detective Gionfriddo would have understood what had frightened and awakened Kathy. Filing his report after the initial investigation the night of the DeFeo murders, Gionfriddo had written that Louise, the mother of the family, had been shot in the head while sleeping on her stomach. Everyone else, including her husband who was lying right beside her, had been shot in the back while lying in the same position. This information had been included in the material turned over to the Suffolk County prosecution team, but never released to the news media. In fact, this detail had never come out, even at Ronnie DeFeo's trial.

Now, Kathy Lutz also knew how Louise DeFeo had died that night. She was in the very same bedroom.

George held his shaken wife in his arms until she had calmed down and fallen back to sleep. Then once again, the urge to check out the boathouse came over him, and George quietly slipped from the room.

He was almost upon Harry in his compound, when the dog awoke, springing to his feet. "Shhh, Harry. It's all right. Take it easy, boy."

The dog settled back on his haunches and watched George test the boathouse door. It was closed and locked. Once more he reached down and reassured Harry. "It's all right, boy. Go back to sleep." George turned and started back toward the house.

George circled around the swimming pool fence. The orb of the full moon was like a huge flashlight, lighting his way. He looked up at the house and stopped short. His heart leaped. From Missy's second floor bedroom window, George could see the little girl staring at him, her eyes following his movements. "Oh, God!" he whispered aloud. Directly behind his daughter, frighteningly visible to George, was the face of a pig. He was sure he could see little red eyes glaring at him!

"Missy!" he yelled. The sound of his own voice broke the grip of terror on his heart and body. George ran for the house. He pounded up the stairs to Missy's bedroom and turned on the light.

She was in bed, lying on her stomach. He went to her and bent over. "Missy?" There was no answer. She was fast asleep.

There was a creak behind him. He turned. Beside the window that looked out at the boathouse, Missy's little chair was slowly rocking back and forth!

Six hours later, at 9:30 in the morning, George and Kathy sat in the kitchen, drinking coffee, confused and upset with the events that were taking place in their new home. They had gone over some of the incidents each had witnessed, and now were trying to put together what was real and what they might have imagined. It was too much for them.

It was December 25, 1975, Christmas Day all over America. The promised white Christmas hadn't materialized as yet for Amityville, but it was cold enough to snow at any moment. Inside, their three children were in the living room, playing near the tree with what few toys George and Kathy had managed to accumulate before moving in eight days earlier.

George figured out that in the first week, he had burned over 100 gallons of oil and an entire cord of logs. Someone would have to go and buy more wood and a few groceries such as milk and bread.

He had told Kathy about trying to reach Father Mancuso on the telephone after the priest had warned him about the sewing room. Now Kathy dialed his number herself and got no answer. She reasoned that

61

the priest might not be in his apartment because of the holiday and could be visiting his own family. Then she volunteered to go for the wood and food.

There was no question as to where Father Mancuso was on this Christmas Day. He was in the Long Island rectory, still suffering. It had not disappeared in the twenty-four hours forecast by the doctor, and his fever had not gone below 103 degrees.

The priest roamed his rooms like a caged lion. An energetic worker who loved the long hours he devoted to his calling, Father Mancuso refused to remain in bed. He had a briefcase full of files; those that he had to deal with as a family counsellor, and those of some of his parish clients. In spite of the Pastor's request that he rest, the priest would put in a full day on Christmas. Above all, Father Mancuso could not shake the uneasiness he felt about the Lutzes and their house.

George heard Kathy return from her shopping. He could tell she was backing the van in because of the grinding sound the snow tires made in the driveway. For some strange reason, the noise bothered him and he became annoyed with his wife.

He went out to meet her, took two logs from the van, put them into the fireplace, and then sat down in the living room, refusing to unload any more. Kathy fumed. George's attitude and appearance were getting on her nerves. Somehow she could sense they were heading for a fight, but she held her tongue for the moment. She took the bags of groceries from the van and left the remaining logs stacked inside. If George felt cold enough, Kathy knew, he'd go get them himself.

She and George had cautioned Danny, Chris, and

Missy to stay out of the sewing room on the second floor, without giving them any reason. That made the children even more curious about what might lie hidden behind the now closed door.

"It could be more Christmas presents," Chris suggested.

Danny agreed, but Missy said, "I know why we have to keep out. Jodie's in there."

"Jodie? Who's Jodie?" asked Danny.

"He's my friend. He's a pig."

"Oh, you're such a baby, Missy. You're always making up dumb things," sneered Chris.

At six o'clock that evening, Kathy was preparing supper for her family when she heard the sounds of something tiny and delicate striking against the glass of her kitchen window. It was dark outside, but she could see it was snowing. White flakes were tumbling down through the reflection of the kitchen light, and Kathy stared at them as the rising wind whipped the snow against the pane. "Snow at last," she said.

Christmas and snow: it brought a reassuring sense of familiarity to the troubled woman. She recalled her own childhood days. There always seemed to be snow at Christmas time when she was young. Kathy kept looking at the little snowflakes. Outside, the multicolored lights from neighborhood Christmas trees gleamed through the night. Behind her, the radio was playing Christmas carols. She became peaceful in her happy kitchen nook.

After supper, George and Kathy sat silently in the living room. The Christmas tree was all lit up and George's tree-topping ornament made a beautiful addition to the decorations. Reluctantly he had gone out to the van and brought in more of the wood. There now were six logs in front of the blazing fireplace, just enough to last through the night at the rate George was shoveling them in.

Kathy worked on some of the children's clothes—patching the boys' trousers that were forever wearing through the knees, letting down a few of Missy's denim pants. The little girl was growing taller, and already the hems were above the tops of her shoes.

At nine o'clock, Kathy went up to the third floor playroom to get Missy ready for bed. She heard her daughter's voice coming from her bedroom. Missy was talking out loud, obviously speaking to someone else in the room. At first Kathy thought it was one of the boys, but then she heard Missy say: "Isn't the snow beautiful, Jodie?" When Kathy entered, her daughter was sitting in her little rocker by the window, staring at the falling snow outside. Kathy looked around the bedroom. There was no one there.

"Who're you talking to, Missy? An angel?"

Missy looked around at her mother. Then her eyes went back to a corner of the room. "No, Mama, just Jodie."

Kathy turned her head to follow Missy's glance. There was nothing there but some of Missy's toys on the floor. "*Jodie?* Is that one of your new dolls?"

"No. Jodie's a pig. He's my friend. Nobody can see him but me."

Kathy knew that Missy, like other children of her age, often created people and animals to talk to, so she assumed it was the child's imagination at work again. George had not yet told her of the incident in Missy's room the night before.

There was another surprise waiting for Kathy when

she got to the top floor a few minutes later. Danny and Chris were already in their own bedroom, changing into their pajamas. Usually both boys fought to stay up past ten. This night, at nine-thirty, they were getting ready without being told. Kathy wondered why.

"What's the matter with you two? How come you're not arguing about going to sleep?"

Her sons shrugged, continuing to undress. "It's warmer in here, Mama," Danny said. "We don't want to play in there anymore."

When Kathy checked *in there*, she was struck by the freezing chill in the playroom. No windows were open, yet the room was ice cold. It certainly wasn't uncomfortable in Danny and Chris' bedroom, nor in the hallway. She felt the radiator. It was hot!

Kathy told George about the cold in the upstairs playroom. Too comfortable by the fireplace to want to move, he said he'd check it out in the morning. At midnight, Kathy and George finally went to bed.

The snow had stopped falling in Amityville, as it had fifteen miles away outside the windows of the Long Island rectory. Father Mancuso turned away from his window. His head hurt. His stomach pained from the flu cramps. The priest was perspiring, and the feeling of suffocating heat made him take off his bathrobe. When he did remove the robe, he began to shiver with a fit of uncontrollable chills.

Father Mancuso couldn't wait to get back into bed. It was cold under the blanket, and he realized he could see his breath in the air. "What the hell's going on?" he muttered to himself. The priest reached out to touch the radiator next to his bed. There was absolutely no heat.

The sick man now felt his body starting to sweat again. Father Mancuso burrowed deep under the blanket, curling up in a tight ball. He closed his eyes and began to pray.

8 December 26 — One night—George doesn't remember exactly which—he woke again at 3:15 in the morning. He dressed and went out, and as he was wandering around in the freezing darkness, he wondered what in God's name he was looking for in the boathouse. Harry, their tough half-breed watchdog, didn't even wake up when George stumbled over some loose wire near Harry's compound.

When the Lutzes lived in Deer Park, Harry also had his own doghouse and slept outside in all kinds of weather. Normally he would remain awake, on guard, until two or three in the morning before finally settling down and going to sleep. Any unfamiliar noise would bring Harry to alert attention. Since they had moved to 112 Ocean Avenue, the dog was usually fast asleep whenever George went out to the boathouse. He would awake only when his master called to him.

George vividly remembers the day after Christmas, however, because that was the date set for Jimmy's wedding. It was also the beginning of a severe case of diarrhea he developed after checking out the boathouse. The pain was intense at first, almost as if a knife had pierced his stomach. George became frightened when he felt nausea rising in his throat. As soon as he re-entered the house, he made a dash for the bathroom on the first floor.

It was daylight outside when he settled back into bed. The abdominal cramps were intense, but finally he fell asleep out of sheer exhaustion. Kathy awoke a few moments later and immediately roused him to remind him of the wedding affair that evening. There would be a lot of arrangements to be handled before her brother came to pick them up. She would be busy with her clothes and hair. George groaned in his half-sleep.

Before going down to prepare breakfast for herself and the children, Kathy went up to the third floor to check the playroom. In was still cold inside when she opened the door, but not as icy as the day before. George might not like to move from his fire, but he would just have to in order to check the radiator. It was working all right, but there was no heat in the room. Certainly the children couldn't stay in there any length of time, and Kathy wanted them out of the way until it was time for them to dress for the wedding. She looked out of the window and saw the ground covered with slush from the melted snow. That settled it. The three would remain indoors today. She decided they would have to play in their own bedrooms.

After they were fed, Missy obediently started up to her own bedroom. Kathy warned her that she was not to go into the sewing room; that she was not even to open the door. "That's okay, Mama. Jodie wants to play in my room today."

"That's my good girl," Kathy smiled. "You go and play with your friend."

The boys wanted to play outside, arguing that this was *their* Christmas vacation from school. It was the way they persisted and answered her back that angered Kathy. Danny and Chris never questioned her requests before this, and she was becoming more aware that her two sons had also changed since they had been in the new house.

But Kathy was not yet aware of her own personality changes, her impatience and crankiness.

"That's enough out of both of you!" she yelled at her sons. "I see you're asking for another beating! Now shut your mouths and get to your room like I said, and stay there until I call you! You hear me? Scat! Upstairs!"

Suddenly, Danny and Chris mounted the stairs to the third floor, passing George on his way down. He didn't acknowledge them. They didn't say good morning to him.

In the dinette, George took one sip of coffee, clutched his stomach, and headed back upstairs to his bathroom. "Don't forget you've got to shave and shower today!" Kathy yelled after him. Considering George's speed in running up the stairs she wasn't sure he had heard her.

Kathy returned to her breakfast nook. She had been

making up a shopping list, checking items in the refrigerator and cabinets that had to be replaced. Food was again running low, and she knew she just had to get herself up and out of the house. She couldn't depend on George to do it. The big freezer in the basement, one of the free items they had received from the DeFeo estate, was clean and could be filled with meat and frozen foods. Her cleaning materials were almost exhausted, since she had been scrubbing the toilet bowls day after day. Most of the blackness was gone by now.

Kathy planned to go to an Amityville supermarket the next morning, Saturday. She wrote "orange juice" on her pad. Suddenly she became aware of a presence in the kitchen. In Kathy's current state of mind over the eroding situation of her family, the memory of the first touch on her hand flooded back, and she froze. Slowly, Kathy looked over her shoulder.

She could see the kitchen was empty—but at the same time, she sensed that the presence was closer, almost directly behind her chair! Her nostrils caught a sweetish scent of perfume, and she recognized it as the odor that had permeated her bedroom four days before.

Startled, Kathy could actually feel a body pressing against hers, clasping its arms around her waist. The pressure was light, however, and Kathy realized that as before, it was a woman's touch—almost reassuring. The unseen presence didn't giver her a sense of danger —not at first.

Then the sweet smell became heavier. It seemed to swirl in the air, making Kathy dizzy. She started to gag, then tried to pull away from a grip that tightened as she struggled. Kathy thought she heard a whisper, and she recalls something deep within her warning her not to listen.

"No!" she shouted. "Leave me alone!" She struck out at the empty air. The embrace tightened, hesitated. Kathy felt a hand on her shoulder, making the same motions of motherly reassurance she had felt the first time in her kitchen.

Then it was gone! All that remained was the odor of the cheap perfume.

Kathy slumped back into her chair and closed her eyes. She began to cry. A hand touched her shoulder. Kathy jumped. "Oh, God, no! Not again!" She opened her eyes.

Missy was standing there, calmly patting her on the arm. "Don't cry, Mama." Then Missy turned her head to look back at the kitchen doorway.

Kathy looked too. But there was nothing there.

"Jodie says you shouldn't cry," Missy said. "He says everything will be all right soon."

At nine that morning, Father Mancuso had awakened in the Long Island rectory and taken his temperature. The thermometer had still read 103 degrees. But at eleven o'clock, the priest suddenly felt better. The cramps had disappeared from his stomach and his head felt clear for the first time in days. Hurriedly he slipped the thermometer back under his tongue: 98.6 degrees. His fever was gone!

Suddenly Father Mancuso felt hungry. He wanted to eat ravenously, but knew he should ease back into his normal diet. The priest made tea and toast in his kitchenette, his mind ticking off all the things that had been backlogged from his heavy work schedule. He forgot completely about George Lutz.

By the same time, eleven A.M., George Lutz had no thoughts for Father Mancuso, Kathy, or his brother-in-law's wedding. He had just made his tenth trip to the bathroom, his diarrhea unrelieved.

Jimmy's wedding and reception, an expensively catered affair for fifty couples, was to be held at the Astoria Manor in Queens. George would have a lot to do at the hall, but right now he couldn't have cared less.

He dragged himself back down the stairs to his chair by the fireplace. Kathy came into the living room to tell him his office in Syosset had telephoned. The men wanted to know when George planned on coming in to work. There were surveying jobs that needed his supervision, and more and more of the building contractors were beginning to complain.

Kathy also wanted to tell him about the second eerie incident in the kitchen, but George waved her off. She knew it would be pointless to try and reach him. Then, from upstairs, she heard the noise of Danny and Chris fighting in their bedroom again, both boys screaming at each other.

She was about to shout up the staircase at them when George bolted past her, mounting the steps two at a time.

Kathy couldn't bring herself to go after her husband. She stood by the bottom of the stairs and listened to George's shouts. In a few minutes there was silence. Then the door to Danny and Chris' bedroom slammed and she heard George's footsteps coming back down. He stopped when he saw Kathy waiting. They looked at each other, but neither spoke. George turned and went back up to the second floor, slamming the door to his and Kathy's bedroom.

George came down a half-hour later. For the first time in nine days, he had shaved and showered. Dressed in clean clothes, he walked into the kitchen where Kathy was sitting with Missy. The little girl was eating lunch. "You get her and the boys ready by five," he said. Then George turned and walked out.

At five-thirty, Jimmy came to pick up his sister and his best man, and the children. They were due at the Astoria Manor by seven. From Amityville to Queens, the Sunrise Highway was the fastest way, and the trip to Astoria normally took an hour at most. The roads were reported to be icy from the recent light snow, however, and it was a Friday night. Traffic would be heavy and slow. Jimmy had played it safe by arriving early at the Lutzes'.

The young bridegroom looked resplendent in his military uniform, his bright face shining with happiness. His sister kissed him excitedly and invited him into the kitchen to wait while George finished dressing.

Jimmy took off his raincoat and then, from his coat pocket, proudly pulled out an envelope packed with fifteen hundred dollars in cash. He had paid out most of the money at the Manor some months before; this was the balance due. He said he had just withdrawn the money from his savings account and it just about wiped him out. Jimmy put the money back into the envelope and returned it to his raincoat pocket, leaving the coat on the kitchen chair beside him.

George came down, neatly clad in a tuxedo. His face was pale from the diarrhea, but he was freshly combed, his dark blonde beard framing his handsome face. The two men went into the living room. George had let the last of his fire burn itself out, and now he poked around the ashes looking for any leftover embers to tamp out.

The children were dressed and ready. Kathy went upstairs to get her coat. When she came down, Jimmy disappeared into the kitchen to get his raincoat. He returned a moment later, hoisting it over his shoulders. "Ready?" George asked.

"Ready as I'll ever be," Jimmy answered, automatically patting his side pocket to check on the envelope of money. His expression froze. He shoved his hand into the pocket, it came out empty! Jimmy searched the other pocket. Again, nothing. He tore off the raincoat, shaking it, then turned out every pocket in his uniform. The money was gone!

Jimmy ran back into the kitchen, Kathy and George following. The three looked all over the room, then began an inch by inch search of the foyer and living room. It was impossible, but Jimmy's fifteen hundred had completely disappeared!

Jimmy became frantic. "George, what am I going to do?"

His brother-in-law put his harm around the distraught Jimmy's shoulder. "Take it easy. The money must be around here somewhere." George moved Jimmy to the door. "Come on, we're running late now. I'll look again when I come back. It's here, don't worry."

Everything just welled up within Kathy and she let go, crying. As George looked at his wife, the lethargy that had gripped him over the past week fell away. He realized how hard he had been on Kathy; for the first time he wasn't thinking only of himself. Then, in spite of the calamity that had just befallen Jimmy, regardless of the weakness he still felt in his loins from the diarrhea, George wanted to make love to Kathy. He hadn't touched her since they had moved into 112 Ocean Avenue. "Come on, honey. Let's go." He gave his wife a pat on her behind. "I'll take care of everything."

George, Kathy and Jimmy got into Jimmy's car; the boys and Missy clambered into the back seat. After closing the door, George stepped out again. "Just a minute. I want to check Harry."

He crossed to the rear of the house. As he walked in the winter's darkness, George called out, "Harry! You keep your eyes open, you hear!"

There was no answering bark. George came up to the wire fence of the compound. "Harry? You there?"

By the reflection of a neighbor's light, he saw that Harry was in his doghouse. George unlatched the gate and entered the compound. "What's the matter, Harry, you sick?"

George bent down. He heard slow canine snoring. It was only six in the evening, and Harry was fast asleep!

9 December 27 — The Lutzes returned home from the wedding at three A.M. It had been a very long night. It began with the mysterious disappearance of Jimmy's fifteen hundred dollars, and several other incidents during the evening hadn't added any particular joy to George's appreciation of the happy event.

Before the wedding ceremony, George, the other ushers, and the bridegroom had taken Communion in a little church near the Manor. During the ritual, George became violently nauseated. When Father Santini, the Pastor of Our Lady of Martyrs Roman Catholic Church, gave George the chalice of wine to drink,

George started to sway dizzily in front of the priest. Jimmy reached out a hand to his brother-in-law, but George brushed it off and dashed toward the men's room at the rear of the church.

After he had thrown up and returned to the hotel, George told Kathy he had actually become queasy the moment he had entered Our Lady of Martyrs.

The reception ran fairly smoothly. There was plenty of the food, drinking, and dancing usually associated with an Irish wedding, and everyone seemed to be having a good time. George had to go to the bathroom only once, when he thought his diarrhea might be returning, but generally he wasn't too uncomfortable. Kathy's brother and his new bride, Carey, were leaving for their honeymoon in Bermuda directly from the Manor and would take a cab to LaGuardia Airport. George would be driving Kathy and the children to Amityville in Jimmy's car, so he didn't drink too much.

Then came the unpleasant moment of settling up with the hall's catering manager. Jimmy, his new father-in-law, and George told the man of the unexpected loss of all the cash, but promised they would pay him his money out of their wedding gifts. Unfortunately, when the traditional "Congratulations are in order" was spoken, most of the envelopes left on the table in front of the bride and groom contained personal checks. The actual cash amounted to a little more than five hundred dollars.

The manager was upset, but after a few minutes of haggling, agreed to accept two checks from George for five hundred dollars each—one from his personal checking account, and the other drawn on George's surveying company's account in Syosset.

George knew he didn't have the five hundred in his

personal checking account, but since the next two days were Saturday and Sunday, he would have time to cover the draft on Monday.

Jimmy's father-in-law quickly conferred with his relatives and scraped up enough cash for his new son-in-law to pay for the honeymoon. Luckily, the plane tickets were already paid for. The wedding party broke up around two, and the Lutzes headed back to 112 Ocean Avenue.

Kathy went up to bed immediately while George checked on the boathouse and the dog's compound. Harry was still asleep, stirring only slightly when George called his name. When he bent to pat the dog, George wondered if Harry was drugged, but then dismissed the thought. No, he was probably just sick. Must have eaten something he found in the yard. George straightened up. He'd have to take Harry to the vet.

The boathouse door was secure, so George returned to the house, locking the front door. As he went to the kitchen, he glanced down at the floor, hoping to spot the missing envelope of money. No luck.

The kitchen door and windows on the first floor were all locked. George climbed the stairs to his bedroom, thinking about his wife and their warm, soft bed. Passing the sewing room, he noticed the door was slightly ajar. He thought of the children. One of them must have opened it before they left the house. He'd ask them the next morning, when they woke up.

Kathy was sleepy, but waiting for him. During the evening she had gotten her husband's vibrations and was eager for his touch. George hadn't touched her since they had moved in. Usually they had made love once a night from the day they were married in July, but from December 18 to December 27, George hadn't made a move in her direction. But now the children were fast asleep, exhausted from their late evening. She watched George undress, and all the misgivings of the past few days melted from her mind.

He slipped under the heavy blanket. "Hey, this is wonderful!" George reached for Kathy's warmth. "Alone at last, as they say."

That night, Kathy had a dream of Louise DeFeo and a man making love in the very same room she was lying in. When she awoke in the morning, the vision remained with her. Somehow Kathy knew that the man was not Louise's husband. It was not until several weeks after she and her family had fled from 112 Ocean Avenue that she learned from an attorney close to the DeFeos that Louise actually did have a lover, an artist who lived with the family for a while. Mr. DeFeo must have known about the affair and informed the lawyer.

In the morning, Kathy took the van to go shopping in Amityville while George drove the children in Jimmy's car to pick up the mail at his office in Syosset. He even gave Harry a ride, telling his employees he would be in on Monday for sure.

They came home to find Kathy putting groceries into the kitchen refrigerator. She had also brought back a load for the basement freezer. Kathy bemoaned the fact that prices were higher in Amityville stores. "I thought they would be," George shrugged. "Amityville is more affluent than Deer Park."

By then it was after one o'clock. Though Kathy wanted to make lunch, she still had to transport the additional frozen foods and meat into her freezer in the basement. George volunteered to put together sandwiches for himself and the children.

While Kathy was in the basement, the front door bell rang. It was her Aunt Theresa. George had met the woman once before at his mother-in-law's, before he and Kathy were married. Theresa had been a nun at one time. Now she had three children, but George never did learn the exact reasons for her departure from her order.

Now the former nun stood in the doorway, a short, thin woman in her early thirties, plainly clad in a worn black wool winter coat and galoshes. Her face was tired but ruddy from the cold. The weather was bright and clear, the temperatures hovering in the low teens. Theresa told George she had taken the bus to Amityville and walked from the station.

George called down to Kathy that her aunt had come to visit. She said she'd be right up, and told George to show Aunt Theresa around her new home.

The children greeted their great-aunt silently. Theresa's grim face forestalled their natural inclination toward friendliness. Danny asked to go outside with Chris. "Okay," George agreed, "but you have to promise to stay within range of the house." Missy ran down the stairs to the basement. George noted how sad Theresa looked when the children didn't respond to her.

As he conducted Theresa around the first floor, pointing out the formal dining room and the huge living room, George became aware of a chill in the house —a clamminess he hadn't noticed until Aunt Theresa came. She agreed that it had seemed rather cold when she entered the house. George looked at the thermostat. It read 75 degrees, but George knew he'd have to kindle the fire again.

They went up to the second floor. Theresa glanced

disapprovingly at the smoked mirrors behind George and Kathy's bed. He could read her thoughts—she believed that such a blatant display smacked of vulgarity —and wanted to tell her that the DeFeos had left the mirrors. But he decided to let the subject pass. The woman was still a nun at heart!

Theresa followed George to the other rooms. She admired all the new space they had, but when she and George stood outside the sewing room, Aunt Theresa hesitated. George opened the door for her. She backed up a few feet, her face turning pale.

"I won't go in there," she said, turning her back to him.

Had Theresa seen anything through the open door? George looked into the room. There were no flies, thank God, or Kathy's reputation for housecleaning would have suffered an irreparable blow! But George could feel the room was ice cold. He looked at Theresa. She was still standing implacably, her back to the room. He shut the door and suggested they try the top floor.

When it came time to examine the playroom, the former nun balked again. "No," she said, "that's another bad place. I don't like it."

Just as George and her Aunt came down, Kathy came up from the basement with Missy. The two women hugged each other, and Kathy, guiding her aunt toward the kitchen, said, "George, I'll finish up downstairs later. I want to transfer some of the canned goods into a closet I found down there. We can use it as a pantry." George went to the living room to build up his fire again.

Theresa hadn't been in the house for more than a half hour when she decided it was time to go. Having expected that her aunt would stay for supper, Kathy was disappointed. "George can drive you back," Kathy offered. But the older woman refused. "There's something bad in here, Kathy," she said, looking about. "I must go now."

"But Aunt Theresa, it's so very cold out." The woman shook her head. She stood up, pulled her heavy coat about her and was heading for the front door when Danny and Chris came in with another young boy.

The three children watched Theresa nod to George and kiss Kathy lightly on the cheek. As she strode out the door, Kathy and George looked at each other, at a loss for words at the woman's strange behavior. Finally Kathy noticed her sons and their playmate.

"This is Bobby, Mama," Chris said. "We just met him. He lives up the street."

"Hello, Bobby," Kathy smiled. The little dark-haired boy looked about Danny's age. Hesitantly, Bobby stuck out his right hand. Kathy shook it and introduced George. "This is Mr. Lutz."

George grinned at the boy, shaking his small hand. "Why don't you three all go upstairs and play?"

Bobby paused, his eyes darting about the foyer. "No. That's all right," he said. "I'd rather play down here."

"*Here*?" asked Kathy. "In the foyer?"

"Yes, ma'am."

Kathy looked at George. Her eyes carried the unspoken question: What's wrong with this house that makes everybody so uncomfortable?

For the next half-hour, the three boys played on the foyer floor, with Danny's and Chris' Christmas toys. Bobby never took off his winter jacket. Kathy went back to the basement to finish making the closet into a pantry, and George returned to the living room fireplace. Then Bobby stood up and told Danny and Chris that he wanted to go home. That was the first and last time that the boy from up the street ever set foot in 112 Ocean Avenue.

The basement of the Lutzes' house was 43 by 28 feet. When George first looked it over, he came down the stairs and saw off to the right batten doors that led to the oil burner, hot water heater, and the freezer, washers, and dryers left from the DeFeo estate.

To his left, through another set of doors, was a play-room, 11 by 28 feet, beautifully finished in walnut paneling, with recessed fluorescent lights in a dropped ceiling. Directly in front of him was the area he planned to use as his office.

A small closet opened into the space beneath the stairs, and between the staircase and the right-hand wall, plywood panels formed an additional closet, extending out about seven feet, with shelving that ran from the ceiling to the floor. This walk-in-area, George thought, made good use of what would otherwise be wasted space, and its proximity to the kitchen stairs made it a most convenient pantry.

Kathy was working in these closets. When she stacked some large, heavy canned goods against the closet's wall, one of the shelves cracked. One side of the plywood paneling on the rear wall seemed to give a little. She moved the cans aside and pushed against the panel. It moved farther away from the shelving.

The closet was lit by a single bulb, hanging from the ceiling. The bulb's reflection shone through a small slit opening just enough to give Kathy the impression that there was an empty space behind the closet, under the tallest section of the stairs. She went out to the basement and called George to come down.

He looked at the opening and pushed against the paneling. The wall continued to give a little more. "There isn't supposed to be anything back there," he said to Kathy.

George removed the four wooden shelves, then shoved hard against the plywood. It swung all the way open. It was a secret door!

The room was small, about four by five feet. Kathy gasped. From the ceiling to floor, it was painted solid red. "What *is* it, George?"

"I don't know," he answered, feeling the three solid concrete block walls. "It seems to be an extra room, maybe a bomb shelter. Everyone was building them back in the late fifties, but it sure doesn't show up in the house plans the broker gave us."

"Do you think the DeFeos built it?" Kathy asked, holding nervously onto George's arm.

"I don't know that either. I guess so," he said, steering Kathy out of the secret room. "I wonder what it was used for." He pulled the panel closed.

"Do you think there are any more rooms like that behind the closets?" Kathy asked.

"I don't know, Kathy," George answered. "I'll have to check out each wall."

"Did you notice the funny smell in there?"

"Yeah, I smelled it," George said. "That's how blood smells."

She took a deep breath. "George, I'm worried about this house. A lot's happening that I don't understand." George saw Kathy put her fingers in her mouth, a sign she was scared. Little Missy always did the same thing when she was frightened. George patted his wife on the head.

"Don't worry, baby. I'll find out what the hell that

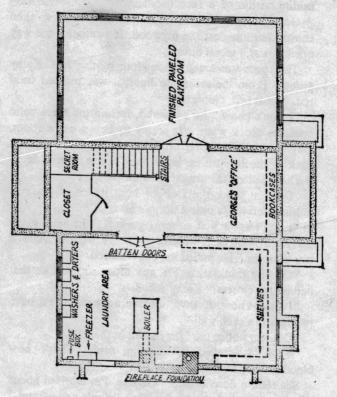

Basement

room is all about. But we *can* use it as an extra pantry!" He turned out the light in the closet, shutting out the sight of the rear wall panel, but not obscuring the fleeting vision of a face he glimpsed against the plywood. In a few days, George would realize it was the bearded visage of Ronnie DeFeo!

10 December 28 — On Sunday, Father Frank Mancuso returned to the Long Island rectory after celebrating Mass in the church. It was only several yards from one building to the other, but the priest felt his recent weakness as he walked in the cold air.

In the Rectory's reception room there was a visitor waiting for him—Sergeant Gionfriddo of the Suffolk County Police Department. The two men shook hands, and Father Mancuso led Gionfriddo to his quarters on the second floor. "I'm glad you called me," the priest said, "and I appreciate that you came."

"That's all right, Father. It's my day off this week." The big detective looked over the priest's apartment.

The living room was filled with books that overflowed the bookcases onto tables and chairs. He took a stack off the couch and sat down.

Father Mancuso wanted to warm up and he had no liquor in his rooms to offer the policeman, so instead he made some tea. While it brewed, he got right to the point of his request for Gionfriddo's visit.

"As you know," he began, "I'm concerned about the Lutzes. That's why I asked Charlie Guarino to contact somebody in Amityville to check if they were all right." The priest walked into the kitchenette to get some cups and saucers. "Charlie reminded me that they're living in the house where that unfortunate DeFeo family was slain. I'd heard about the case from some friends of mine, but I don't really know how it happened."

"I was on that case, Father," the detective interrupted.

"So Charlie told me when he called back the other night." Father Mancuso brought the tea and sat down across from Gionfriddo. "Anyway, I had a hard time falling asleep last night. I don't know why, but I kept thinking about the DeFeos."

He looked up at Gionfriddo, trying to read the expression on his face. It was difficult, even though Father Mancuso had years of experience in probing people for facts, fancied or real; from his clients in family counseling who came before him. He didn't know whether to reveal what had happened to him on the first day in 112 Ocean Avenue or on the telephone to George.

Gionfriddo quickly read the priest's thoughts and solved the problem. "You think there's something funny going on in that house, Father?"

"I don't know. That's what I wanted to ask you."

The detective put down his cup of tea. "What is it

you're looking for? A haunted house? You want me to tell you there's something spooky about the place?"

The priest shook his head. "No, but it'll help me if you can tell me what happened the night of the murders. I understand the boy said he heard voices."

Gionfriddo looked into a pair of piercing eyes and saw the priest was troubled. He cleared his throat and put on his official voice. "Well, basically, the story is that Ronald DeFeo drugged his family at dinner on November 13, 1974, and then shot them all with a high-powered rifle while they were out cold. At his trial, he did claim a voice told him to do it."

Father Mancuso waited for more details, but Gionfriddo had finished his report. "That's it?" the priest asked.

Gionfriddo nodded. "Like I said, that's it, basically."

"It must have awakened the whole neighborhood?" Father Mancuso continued.

"No. Nobody heard the shots. We found out about it later when Ronnie went into The Witches' Brew and told the bartender. The Witches' Brew is a bar near Ocean Avenue. The kid was stoned out of his head."

Father Mancuso was confused. "You mean he used a high-powered rifle to kill six people, and no one heard all that noise?"

Gionfriddo thinks it was just about then that he began to feel nauseous in the priest's apartment. He felt he had to leave. "That's right. People in houses on both sides of the DeFeos said they never heard a thing that night." Gionfriddo stood up.

"Isn't that rather peculiar?"

"Yeah, I thought so myself," the detective said, slipping on his overcoat. "But you got to remember, Father, it was the middle of winter. A lot of people sleep with their windows shut tight. At 3:15 in the morning, they're dead to the world."

Sergeant Al Gionfriddo knew the priest had more questions, but he didn't care. He had to get out of there. No sooner was he outside the Rectory than he threw up.

By the time he returned to Amityville, Gionfriddo felt the uneasiness passing. At first he thought of driving past 112 Ocean Avenue, but changed his mind. Instead he headed home, rolling up Amityville Road. He drove past The Witches' Brew on his right.

The Witches' Brew was a hangout for a lot of kids in town, especially during the season when Amityville was filled with summer-house renters. But now, on a December Sunday afternoon, Amityville Road, the main shopping street in town, was empty. The pro-football playoffs were on television and the regulars were at home, glued to their sets.

As he rode by, Gionfriddo didn't really notice the figure going into The Witches' Brew. The detective was a good fifty feet beyond before he swerved his police car and braked to a stop. He looked back, but the man was gone. The shape of the body, the beard, and the swaggering walk were the same as Ronnie DeFeo's!

Gionfriddo continued to stare at the doorway to the club. "Agh! I'm getting jumpy," he muttered. "Who needs that priest?" The detective turned around, jerked the gear shift into drive and pulled away from the curb, burning rubber like a hot rodder.

Inside The Witches' Brew, George Lutz ordered his first beer. He wondered why the bartender stared at him when he sat down at the bar. The man opened a bottle of Miller's and was pouring it when he stopped. He looked as though he was about to say something to George, but then went ahead pouring the beer.

George looked around him. The Witches' Brew could have been any one of a number of bars George had seen in his travels as a Marine corporal and as a surveyor working the small towns and villages of Long Island: dimly lit, the usual garish juke box, the smell of stale beer and smoke. There was just one other customer in the place, down at the very end of the long mahogany bar, absorbed by watching a television set above the bar mirror as an announcer described the first-half action of the football game.

George sniffed, took a gulp of his beer and looked at himself in the mirror behind the bar. He'd had to get out of the house for a while, be by himself. He couldn't get a handle on what was happening to his family. The little bits and pieces that he would recognize later on were still too isolated for him.

George couldn't understand what was wrong with the children since they moved into the new house. In his eyes, they were wild, unmannered. That had never been the case before, not when they lived in Deer Park.

He thought Missy was acting strangely. Did he really see a pig in her window the other night? And where was Jimmy's money? How could it simply disappear in front of them?

George finished his beer and signaled for another. His eyes returned to his image in the mirror. He recalled now, earlier that week, he'd been sitting like a dummy in front of the fireplace, then standing and staring in the boathouse. Why? And now this business with that red room in the basement. What the hell was that all about?

Well, tomorrow he'd begin to dig into the background of his house. The first place to do that would be the Amityville Real Estate Tax Assessment Office, where he could look at the record of improvements that applied to the property at 112 Ocean Avenue.

"Yeah," he muttered to himself, "and I got to get to the bank and cover that check. Can't let that bounce." George drank down the last of his second beer. At first he didn't notice the bartender standing in front of him. Then he looked up and saw the man waiting. George covered his glass with his hand to signal that he didn't want another.

"Excuse me, mister,'" said the bartender. "You passing through?"

"No," answered George. "I live here in Amityville. We just moved in."

The bartender nodded. "Well, you are a dead ringer for a young feller from around here. For a moment I thought you was him." He rang up George's money. "He's away now. Won't be back for a while." He put the change on the bar. "Maybe never."

George took the money and shrugged. People were always mistaking him for someone else they knew. Maybe it was the beard. A lot of guys wore them these days. "Well, see you around." He headed for the entrance to The Witches' Brew.

The bartender nodded again. "Yeah, drop in again."

George was at the door. "Hey!" asked the bartender. "By the way, where'd you move into?"

George stopped, looked back, and pointed toward the general direction of the west. "Oh, just a couple of streets from here. On Ocean."

The bartender felt George's used beer glass slipping

from his hand. When he heard George's final remark, "112 Ocean Avenue," it dropped from his hand and crashed on the floor.

Kathy was waiting for George to come home. She sat in the living room by the Christmas tree, not wanting to be in the kitchen nook by herself for fear of meeting up with that invisible something that reeked of perfume. The children were up in the boys' bedroom, watching television. They had been quiet most of the afternoon, absorbed in an old movie. By the delighted laughter that drifted down to her, Kathy was sure it was Abbott and Costello.

Now she was trying to concentrate on where Jimmy's money could be. Again Kathy and George had gone over every square inch of the kitchen, foyer, living and dining rooms, and closets looking for the envelope. It *couldn't* just have vanished into thin air! No one could have possibly been in the house to take it. Where the devil could it have gone?

Kathy thought about the presence in the kitchen and shuddered. She forced her mind to think of other rooms in the house. The sewing room? The red room in the basement? She began to get out of her chair, then stopped. Kathy was afraid to go down there alone now. Anyway, she thought, sitting back down, she and George hadn't seen anything but the red paint when they were in there.

She looked at her watch. It was almost four o'clock. Where was George? He had been gone over an hour. Then, out of the corner of her right eye, she saw movement.

One of Kathy's first Christmas gifts to George had been a huge, four-foot ceramic lion, crouched, ready to leap upon an unseen victim, and painted in realistic colors. George had thought it a pretty piece and had moved it to the living room, where it now sat on a large table beside his chair near the fireplace.

When Kathy turned and looked fully at the sculpture, she was sure she had seen it move a few inches closer toward her!

After Sergeant Gionfriddo left Father Mancuso's apartment that afternoon, the priest became angry with himself. He hated the way he was handling the Lutz situation and resolved to break his obsession with the whole affair. For the next several hours he dove into issues that were coming up in Court the following week, poring over caseloads that had piled up.

Realizing he had important decisions to make that would affect people's lives, he now cleared his mind of abstractions like Gionfriddo's unsatisfactory explanation of the DeFeo murders and the doubts he had about the Lutzes' safety in that house. As he worked, he slowly became aware that he was regaining his strength. The weakness he had felt in the wintry air was gone. It was now after six, he was hungry, and he reminded himself that he hadn't had anything to eat or drink since that cup of tea with Gionfriddo.

Father Mancuso put down a file, stretched his body, and went into the kitchenette. In the living room, the telephone rang. It was his private number. He picked it up and said "Hello?" There was no answer, only static crackling from the receiver.

The priest felt a chill run through his frame. As he held the telephone in his hand, he began to perspire, recalling his last call with George Lutz.

* * *

George was listening to the sharp, snapping pops on his own telephone. It had rung while he was in the kitchen with Kathy and the children.

Finally, after no one answered his repeated hellos, George slammed the receiver back on the hook.

"How do you like that? Some wise guy's on the other end playing games!"

Kathy looked up at her husband. They were eating supper, George had shown up just a few moments before. He told her he had taken a very long walk around the town and he was convinced the street they lived on in Amityville was the nicest.

Kathy thought George looked better for having gotten out of the house. She felt foolish about wanting to mention the lion and forgot the incident now that George was upset again. "What happened?" she asked.

"There was no one on the other end, that's what happened. It was just a lot of static." He started to sit down again at the table.

"You know, it was just like the other time when I tried to talk to Father Mancuso. I wonder if he's trying to reach us?" George went back to the telephone and dialed the priest's private number.

He waited until it had rung ten times. There was no answer. George looked at the electric clock over the kitchen sink. It was exactly seven. He shivered a little. "Don't you think it's getting chilly in here again, Kathy?"

Father Mancuso had just taken his temperature. It was up to 102 degrees. "Oh, no," he moaned, "not that again!" He began to take his pulse, holding a finger on his wrist. The priest started to count when the big hand of his watch was exactly on twelve. He noted it was seven o'clock.

In one minute's time, his heart beat one hundred and twenty times! Normally Father Mancuso's pulse ran about 80 beats per minute. He knew he was going to be sick again.

George left the kitchen for the living room. "I'd better put some more wood into the fireplace," he told Kathy.

She watched her husband shamble out of the kitchen. Kathy began to get that depressed feeling again. Then she heard a loud crash from the living room. It was George!

"Who the hell left this goddamned lion on the floor? It almost killed me!"

11 December 29 to 30 — The next morning, Monday, George's ankle was stiff. He had taken a nasty tumble over the porcelain lion and fallen heavily against some of the logs by the fireplace. He also had a cut over his right eye, but it hadn't bled much after Kathy put a Band-Aid on it. What disturbed Kathy was the clear imprint of teethmarks on his ankle!

George limped out to his 1974 Ford van and had trouble turning over the cold motor. With temperatures in the low twenties, George knew he could anticipate ignition problems. But finally he got the van going and headed across the Island toward Syosset. His first order of business was to cover the check he had written to the Astoria Manor. That meant drawing funds from the account of William H. Parry, Inc., his land surveying business.

Halfway to Syosset, on the Sunrise Highway, George felt a bump in the back of the van. He pulled over and inspected the rear end. One of the shock absorbers had come loose and fallen off. George was puzzled. This was a mishap that might occur after the shocks were old and worn, if then, but the Ford had gone only 26,000 miles. He drove on again intending to replace the part once he returned to Amityville.

After George drove off that morning, Kathy's mother called to tell her that she had received a card from Jimmy and Carey in Bermuda. "Why don't you bring the children over to my house for a while?" Jimmy's car was still in the driveway, but Kathy didn't feel like leaving home. She said she still had a load of laundry to do, but that she and George might come over New Year's Eve. They had made no plans as yet, and she would ask George when he came back.

Kathy hung up and looked around, feeling at a loss as to what she should do next. The depressed feeling from the day before was still with her, and she was afraid to remain alone in the kitchen or go down to the washing machines in the basement. After the ceramic lion incident, Kathy also hesitated about going into the living room. She finally wound up going upstairs to be near the children. With them, she thought, she wouldn't feel so alone and frightened.

Kathy looked in on Missy in her bedroom and Danny and Chris in theirs before going into her own room and lying down. She had been on the bed, dozing, for about fifteen minutes, when she began to hear noises coming from the sewing room across the hall. It sounded as if someone was opening and closing a window.

Kathy got off the bed and went to the sewing room door. It was still shut. She could see that Missy was in her own bedroom and she could hear the boys running around on the floor above.

She listened. Behind the closed door, the sounds continued. Kathy stared at the door, but did not dare open it. She turned around and went back to her bedroom and got back on the bed, pulling the cover up over her head.

In Syosset, George found a caller waiting for him. The man introduced himself as an inspector from the Internal Revenue Service and explained he was there to examine the company's books and past tax returns. George called his accountant. The IRS agent spoke with him and made an appointment to return on January 7th.

After the agent left, George got on with his priorities: withdrawing five hundred dollars from the William H. Parry, Inc., account and depositing it in his personal checking account; going over the plans that had been completed for several land surveys; deciding how to handle the few assignments that had come into the office since he had been away; and then doing some research into the DeFeo family and the background of 112 Ocean Avenue.

When the men on his staff asked him why he'd been out so long, George told them only that he had been sick. He knew that was untrue, but what other explanation would make any sense? By one o'clock, George had completed his duties in Syosset. He planned to make one more stop before heading back to Amityville.

Long Island's largest daily newspaper, in pages of advertising and circulation, is *Newsday*. George reasoned that if there was any place where he could learn some facts about the DeFeos, *Newsday*'s Garden City office would be the most logical starting point.

He was referred to the microfilm department, where a clerk checked the cross-index files for the dates of the DeFeo murders and Ronnie's trial. George only vaguely recalled the details of the way the son had slaughtered the whole family, but he did remember that the trial had been held in Riverhead, Long Island, sometime in the fall of 1975.

George put the microfilm of the newspaper into the reader and ran it down until he came to November 14, 1974. One of the first items he noticed was a photograph taken of Ronnie DeFeo at the time of his arrest, the morning after the discovery of his family's bodies at 112 Ocean Avenue. The bearded twenty-four-year-old face staring back at him from the picture could have been his own! He was about to read on, when it hit George that this *was* the face he had seen fleetingly on the closet wall in his basement!

The first articles told how Ronnie had run into a bar near his home, calling for help, saying that someone had killed his parents, brothers, and sisters. With two friends, Ronald DeFeo returned to his house where they found Ronald, Sr., 43; Louise, 42; Allison, 13; Dawn, 18; Mark, 11; and John, 9. All were in their beds, all shot in the back.

The story continued that at the time of DeFeo's arrest the following morning, Amityville police said that the motives for the murders were a $200,000 life insurance policy and a strongbox filled with cash hidden in his parents' bedroom closet.

The last item explained that when the prosecution was ready, the trial would be held in the State Supreme Court at Riverhead.

George inserted another microfilm reel, this one containing the day-by-day record of the seven-week trial held from September through November. The record included charges of police brutality in forcing a confession from Ronnie DeFeo, and went on to attorney William Weber's parading psychiatrists to the stand to substantiate his plea of Ronnie's insanity. However, the jury found the youth sane and guilty of murder. Imposing a sentence of six *consecutive* life terms, State Supreme Court Justice Thomas Salk called the killings the "most heinous and abhorrent crimes."

George left the *Newsday* offices, thinking of the Coroner's report that pinpointed the time of the DeFeos' deaths at about 3:15 in the morning. That was the exact moment George had been waking since they'd been in the house! He would have to tell Kathy.

George also wondered if the DeFeos had used the red room in the basement as a secret hideaway for their money. As he drove back to Amityville, George was so absorbed in thought that he never noticed or heard his left tire wobbling.

As he stopped for a red light on Route 110, another car pulled alongside. The driver leaned over and opened his window on the right side. He tooted his horn to catch George's attention, then yelled that George's wheel was coming off!

George got out and examined the wheel. All the bolts were loose. George could feel them turn easily in his fingers. With his windows closed he had dimly heard the racket, but being wrapped up in his thoughts, he just never considered it was coming from his car.

What the devil was going on? First the shock absorber had fallen off, now this. Was someone fooling around with the van? He or Kathy could be killed if the wheel came off while driving at any speed.

George became even angrier and more frustrated when he looked for the jack handle in the rear of the van. It was gone! He'd have to tighten the bolts by hand until he could get to a service station. By then it would be too late to do any further checking on the background of 112 Ocean Avenue.

On Tuesday Father Mancuso could no longer ignore the redness in the palms of his hands, nor the excruciating pain he felt when he touched the sore spots. Even though the doctor had given him antibiotic injections, he had been unable to shake off this second flu attack. His temperature remained high, and every ache and pain in his body seemed intensified and magnified a hundred-fold.

The day before, Monday, Father Mancuso had accepted the redness that developed in his palms as just another manifestation of his illness. When the peculiar coloring and extreme sensitivity remained and it became painful to pick up anything with his hands, Father Mancuso started to become a great deal more concerned.

The next day, the Amityville Historical Society had some interesting information for George, particularly about the very location of his house. It seems the Shinnecock Indians used land on the Amityville River as an enclosure for the sick, mad, and dying. These unfortunates were penned up until they died of exposure. However, the record noted that the Shinnecocks did not use this tract as a consecrated burial mound because they believed it to be infested with demons.

For how many uncounted centuries the Shinnecocks carried on in this manner, no one really knows; but in the late 1600's, white settlers eased the first Americans out of the area, sending them farther out on Long Island. To this day, Shinnecocks still own land, property, and businesses on the eastern tip of the Island.

One of the more notorious settlers who came to the newly-named Amityville in those days was a John Catchum or Ketcham who had been forced out of Salem, Massachusetts, for practicing witchcraft. John set up residence within 500 feet of where George now lived, continuing his alleged devil worship. The account also claimed he was buried somewhere on the northeast corner of the property.

From the Real Estate Tax Assessment Office in town, George learned that the house at 112 Ocean Avenue had been built in 1928 by a Mr. Monaghan. It passed through several families until 1965, when the DeFeos purchased it from the Rileys. But in spite of all he had read in the past two days, George was no closer to a solution of what the mysterious red room was used for or who built it. There was no record of any improvements being made to the house that resembled the addition of a basement room.

It was the night before New Year's Eve. The Lutzes went to bed early. George had checked the sewing room for Kathy, as he had done the night before after returning from *Newsday*. Both evenings the windows had been shut and locked.

Earlier they had discussed what George had discovered about the history of their property and house. "George," Kathy asked nervously, "do you think it's haunted?"

"No way," he replied. "I don't believe in ghosts. Besides, everything that's happened around here must have a logical and scientific explanation to it."

"I'm not so sure. What about the lion?"

"What about it?" he asked.

Kathy looked around the kitchen where they were sitting. "Well, what about what I felt those two times? I told you I *know* somebody touched me, George."

George stood up, stretching. "Oh, come on, honey, I think it's just your imagination." He reached for her hand. "I've had that happen to me too, when I was sure my father had put his hand on my shoulder in the office." He pulled Kathy out of her chair. "I was positive he was standing right beside me. It happens to a lot of people, but it's, it's—I think they call it clairvoyance, or something like that."

The couple had their arms around each other's waists as George turned out the light in the kitchen. They passed the living room on the way to the stairs. Kathy stopped. She could see the crouching lion in the darkness of the room.

"George. I think we should continue with our meditation. Let's do it tomorrow, okay?"

"You think that way we can find a logical explanation for all that's happened?" he asked, drawing her upstairs.

* * *

There was no logical or scientific explanation for Father Frank Mancuso as he prepared to go to bed. He had just prayed in his own rooms, searching and hoping for an answer to the question of why his palms were itching so terribly.

12 December 31 — The year 1976 was just around the corner. The last day of the old year dawned on a heavy snowfall, and to many people that was the signal that a fresh, clean start would usher in the new.

In the Lutz household, there was a completely different mood. George hadn't slept well, even though he had been active enough for the past two days, inside and outside the house. He awoke during the night, looked at his watch and was surprised to find it was 2:30 A.M., not 3:15, as he anticipated.

George awoke again at 4:30 A.M., saw it was beginning to snow, and tried to fall back to sleep under the warm covers. But, tossing and turning, he couldn't find a comfortable position. In her sleep, Kathy was bothered by his restlessness and rolled over against George so that he was pushed to the edge of the bed. Wide awake, he kept having visions of discovering secret caches of money around the house and using them to solve all his financial problems.

George was beginning to choke with the pressures of mounting bills; for the house he had just taken on, and for the office, where he would shortly have a very serious payroll deficit. All the cash that he and Kathy had saved had gone toward the expense of the closing, an old fuel bill, and paying off the boats and motorcycles. And now the latest blow—the investigation of his books and tax returns by the Internal Revenue Service. Small wonder that George dreamed of a simple magical solution to the bind he was in.

He wished he could find Jimmy's money. The fifteen hundred would be a lifesaver. George stared at the falling snow. He had read in the newspaper account that Mr. DeFeo had been extremely well off, with a big bank account and with a very good position working for his wife's father in a big car dealership.

George had examined his bedroom closet and discovered Mr. DeFeo's secret hiding place under the door jamb. The police had found it first at the time of Ronnie's arrest and now it was empty, just a hole in the floor. He kept wondering where else the DeFeos could have stashed away some of their cash.

The boathouse! George sat up in bed. Maybe there was a meaning behind his being drawn there every night. Was some—some *thing* dragging him there? Was the dead man somehow urging him to look in there for his fortune? George was desperate, he knew, even to contemplate such a screwy idea. But why else *would* he be driven to the boathouse, night after night?

At six-thirty, George finally gave up and got out of bed. He knew he would never fall asleep again that morning, so he quietly slipped from the room, went down to the kitchen, and made some coffee.

It was still dark outside at that hour, but he could see the snow was beginning to pile up near the kitchen door. He saw a light on the ground floor of his neighbor. Maybe the owner also had money problems and couldn't sleep, he thought.

George knew he wouldn't go to the office that day. It was New Year's Eve and everybody would be leaving early anyway. He drank his coffee and planned to search the boathouse and basement for some clues. Then George began to feel a chill in the house.

The thermostat automatically dropped the temperature between midnight and six in the morning. But now it was almost seven and the heat didn't seem to be on. George went into the living room and put some kindling and paper into the fireplace. Before the wood blazed up, George noticed that the brick wall was black from all the soot accumulated from his almost constant fires.

A little after eight, Kathy came down with Missy. The little girl had awakened her mother with delighted squeals. "Oh, Mama, look at all the snow! Isn't it beautiful! I want to go outside and play with my sled today!"

Kathy made her daughter breakfast, but couldn't eat anything herself. She had coffee and a cigarette. George didn't want any food and took only another cup of coffee. He had to get it from the kitchen himself because Kathy didn't want to come into the living room. She told George she had a bad headache. Kathy was frightened of the porcelain lion and planned to get rid of it before the day was out. But it was true that she did have a sick headache.

By nine o'clock, George had built the living room fire to a roaring blaze. At ten o'clock, the snow was still falling. Kathy called out to George from the kitchen that a local radio station had predicted the Amityville River would be completely frozen by nightfall.

Reluctantly, George got up from his chair by the fireplace and dressed, put on his boots, and went out to the boathouse. He hadn't had the money to take the cabin cruiser out of the water for the winter. If the river froze, ice would eventually crush the boat, but he had prepared for just this kind of emergency.

George's mother had given him her paint compressor and he had drilled holes in its plastic hose. Now he sank the hose in the water beside the boat and turned on the compressor. It acted as a bubbler system that would keep the water inside the boathouse from freezing.

All that morning, Father Mancuso had been looking at his hands, which had begun to fester the night before. They were now dry, but angry red blisters remained.

His fever also held at a high of 103°. When the Pastor had looked in on him, Father Mancuso had promised to remain in bed for the rest of the day. The priest did not mention what had been happening to his hands. He kept them in the pockets of his bathrobe.

When the Pastor left his rooms, Father Mancuso stared at the ugly manifestation on his skin, and he became angry. All this suffering for just one appearance in an inconsequential house in Amityville? The priest was prepared to give himself in any way that God demanded, but at least, he thought, let it be to help humanity. With all his training, devotion, experience and skill, certainly there had to be some rational explanation he could apply to the enigma. At the moment he couldn't, and that accounted for his rage.

Along with his anger, the pains in his palms increased. He decided to pray for relief. And as Father Mancuso asked for help, his concentration on his misfortune decreased. The numbness in his tightly gripped hands slowly diminished in its pressure. He spread his fingers and stared at the blisters. The priest sighed and knelt to thank God.

Later in the afternoon was the second time Danny and Chris threatened to run away from home. The first had been when they lived in George's house at Deer Park. He had restricted them to their rooms for a week, because they were lying to him and Kathy about small things. They had revolted against his authority: Both boys refused to obey his orders, threatening to run away if he also forced them to give up television. At that point, George called their bluff, telling Danny and Chris that they could get out if they didn't like the way he ran things at home.

The two youngsters had taken him at his word. They packed all their belongings—toys, clothes, records, and magazines—into bed rolls and dragged the big bundles out the front door. When they were about halfway down the street, desperately trying to move the heavy load, a neighbor spotted them and talked them both into going back. For a while, they stopped their childish fibbing, but now there had come a new eruption.

When she heard them fighting, Kathy had gone up to their room and found the boys on one of the beds. Chris was straddling Danny's chest, ready to clobber his older brother. On the other bed sat Missy, a broad grin on her little face. She was clapping her hands with excitement.

Kathy pulled her sons apart. "What do you think you're doing?" she screamed. "What's the matter with you two? Are you going crazy?"

Missy chimed in, "Danny didn't want to clean up the room like you told him to."

Kathy looked sternly at the boy. "And why not, young man? Do you see what this room looks like?"

The room *was* a mess. Toys were scattered all over the floor, intermingled with discarded clothes. The tubes of an old paint set had been left uncapped, the pigments oozing onto the furniture and rug. Some of their new Christmas toys had already been broken and were discarded in corners of the bedroom. Kathy shook her head. "I don't know what I'm going to do with you. We bought this beautiful house so you'd have your own playroom, and look at what you've done!"

Danny tore himself loose from his mother's grip. "You don't want us to stay in that dumb old playroom!"

"Yeah!" Chris chimed in. "We don't like it around here. There's nobody to play with!"

Kathy and the boys bickered back and forth for another five minutes until Danny threw down the gauntlet and challenged his mother with the threat of running away from home. Kathy, in turn, suggested corporal punishment for their behavior. "And you know who dishes it out around here!"

By dinner time, the Lutz family had settled down. The boys had cooled off, though Kathy could still feel an undercurrent of tension at the table. George had told Kathy he preferred staying home this New Year's Eve rather than facing drunks on the road home from her mother's house. They had made no plans to be with their friends, and it was too cold to go out to a movie.

After they had eaten, Kathy convinced George to move the ceramic lion back up to the sewing room. Again there were some flies clinging to the window pane facing the Amityville River. George angrily swatted them to death before slamming the door shut.

By ten o'clock, Missy had fallen asleep on the living room floor. She had exacted a promise from Kathy to awaken her at midnight in time to blow her party horn. Danny and Chris were still up, playing near the Christmas tree and watching television. George was attending to his fire. Kathy sat across from him, trying to lose her depression by looking at an old movie with the boys.

As the night wore on, Father Mancuso's hands had been acting up again. Now the blisters were worse, breaking out on the backs of his hands. He couldn't put up with the thought of spending the entire night in pain and fright. When his doctor looked in on him, he suddenly shoved his palms out and said, "Look!"

Gently the physician examined the blisters. "Frank, I'm not a dermatologist," he said. "This could be anything from an allergy to an attack of anxiety. Has something been bothering you that badly?"

Father Mancuso turned sadly away from the doctor, his eyes staring out the window at the snow. "I think so. Something. . . ." The priest brought his gaze back to the doctor ". . . or somebody."

The doctor assured the priest that he'd have some relief by the morning. Then he left for a New Year's Eve party.

* * *

On television, Guy Lombardo saluted the New Year from the Waldorf-Astoria Hotel. The Lutzes watched the ball fall from the Allied Chemical Building in Times Square, but did not share the countdown with announcer Ben Grauer while he tolled off the last ten seconds of 1975.

Danny and Chris had gone up to their room about a half hour earlier, their eyes red from too much television and the smoke from George's fire. Kathy had put Missy into her bed and then come back downstairs to her chair across from George.

It was now exactly one minute after twelve. She stared into the fireplace, hypnotized by the dancing flames. Something was materializing in those flames—a white outline against the blackened bricks—becoming clearer, more distinct.

Kathy tried to open her mouth to say something to her husband. She couldn't. She couldn't even tear her eyes away from the demon with horns and a white peaked hood on its head. It was getting larger, looming toward her. She saw that half of its face was blown away, as if hit with a shotgun blast at close range. Kathy screamed.

George looked up. "What's the matter?" he said.

All Kathy could do was to point into the fireplace. George followed her gaze and he saw it too—a white figure that had burned itself into the soot against the rear bricks of the fireplace.

13 January 1, 1976 — George and Kathy finally went to bed at one in the morning. They had been sleeping for what later seemed to them no more than five minutes when they were awakened by a howling wind roaring through their bedroom.

The blankets on the bed had been virtually torn from their bodies, leaving George and Kathy shivering. All the windows in the room were wide open, and the bedroom door, caught by the drafts, was swinging back and forth.

George leaped from the bed and ran to close the windows. Kathy gathered the blankets off the floor and threw them back onto the bed. Both were breathless from their sudden awakening, and even though the door to their room had slammed shut, they could still hear the wind blowing out in the second floor hallway.

George wrenched open the door and was hit by another cold blast. Flipping on the light switch in the hall, he was startled to see the doors to the sewing room and dressing room wide open, the gale rushing freely through the open windows. Only the door to Missy's bedroom remained shut.

He ran into the dressing room first, fighting against the gale that hit him, and managed to force the windows down. Then he went to the sewing room and, with the cold now bringing tears to his eyes, closed one window. But George could not budge the open window that faced the Amityville River. He banged furiously on its frame with his fists. Finally it gave and slid to a close.

He stood there, trying to catch his breath, shaking in his pajamas. The wind was no longer blowing through the house, but he could hear it gusting violently outside. The chill remained. George took one more look around the room before he remembered Kathy. "Honey?" he called out. "You all right?"

When Kathy followed her husband out into the hallway, she too had seen the open doors, and that Missy's door remained shut. Her heart thumping, Kathy had run to her daughter's room and burst through the doorway. She turned on the light.

The room was warm, almost hot. The windows were shut and locked, and the little girl was fast asleep in her bed.

There was something moving in the room. Then she saw it was Missy's chair beside the window, slowly rocking back and forth. Then she heard George's voice. "Honey? You all right?"

George came into the bedroom. The heat struck him; it was like stepping in front of a fire. George took it all in at once—the little girl safely asleep, his wife standing at the side of Missy's bed, the incredulous look of fright on Kathy's face, and the small chair teetering back and forth.

He took one step toward the rocking chair and it immediately ceased its movements. George stopped in his tracks, stood absolutely still, and motioned to Kathy. "Take her downstairs! Hurry!"

Kathy didn't question George. She lifted the little girl off the bed, blankets and all, and hurried from the room. George came out right behind them and slammed the door, not even bothering to turn off the light.

Kathy went carefully down the steps toward the first floor. It was ice cold in the hallway. George ran up the staircase to the top floor where Danny and Chris were sleeping.

When he came back down from the third floor a few minutes later, he saw Kathy sitting in the dark living room. She held Missy in her arms, the little girl still fast asleep on her lap. He turned on the light in the room, the chandelier casting shadows into the corners.

Kathy turned from the fireplace to look up at George questioningly. "They're all right," he nodded. "They're both sleeping. It's cold up there, but they're okay." Kathy let out her breath. He saw its vapor hang in the cold air.

George hurriedly started a fire. His fingers were numb and he suddenly realized that he was barefoot and hadn't thrown anything on over his pajamas. George finally got a small blaze going with newspaper, then fanned the flame with his hand until some of the old kindling caught fire.

Crouched in front of the fireplace, he could hear the winds howling outside. Then he turned and looked at Kathy over his shoulder. "What time is it?"

That was the only thing he could think of to say, George Lutz recalls. He remembers the look on Kathy's face when he asked the question. She stared at him for a moment, then replied, "I think it's about. . . ." But before Kathy could finish, she burst into tears, her whole body shaking uncontrollably. She rocked Missy back and forth in her arms, sobbing. "Oh, George, I'm frightened to death!"

George stood up and walked over to his wife and daughter. He crouched down in front of the chair and put his arms around both. "Don't cry, honey," he whispered. "I'm here. Nobody's going to hurt you or the baby."

The three remained in that position for some time. Slowly the fire burned brighter and the room began to warm up. It seemed to George that the winds were diminishing outside. Then he heard the oil burner click on in the basement and he knew it was exactly six o'clock in the morning on New Year's Day.

By nine A.M., the temperature in 112 Ocean Avenue had risen to the thermostat-controlled 75 degrees. The icy chill in the house had dissipated. George had made an inspection tour of each window, from the first floor to the third. There was no visible evidence that anyone had tampered with the locks on the windows of the second floor, and George remained completely baffled as to how such a bizarre event could have taken place.

Looking back at the episode, he claims that at that time, he and Kathy couldn't think of any reason for the windows behaving the way they did except for a freak of nature—that the hurricane-strength winds had somehow forced the windows up. But he can't answer why it happened only to the second floor windows and not to any others in the house.

Suddenly George felt an urge to go to his office. It was a holiday, no one would be in, but he felt compelled to check on his company's operations.

William H. Parry, Inc., had four crews of engineers and surveyors in the field. The company had created the plans and blueprints for the largest building complex to date in New York City, and for the Glen Oaks Towers in Glen Oaks, Long Island, and was also responsible for planning a forty-block urban renewal project in Jamaica, Queens. In addition, there were several small surveys for title companies. The coordination for setting up each day's work was quite intricate, and for the past few weeks, George had been leaving that assignment to one of the draftsmen—an experienced employee who had worked for his father and grandfather.

Over the past year, after he had taken full control of the company from his mother, George's main concern had been with collecting from the city and construction companies that used his services. The company's payroll and expenses were much larger than they had been when George's father was alive. There was also the matter of paying off six cars and new field equipment. George realized he had been slacking off; it was time to resume his share of the responsibilities.

At ten in the morning, Father Mancuso was also awake. He hadn't slept much and had gotten up several times during the night to soak his blistered hands in

Burow's Solution as the doctor had recommended. The priest had been out of bed since seven, even though he was enervated by flu and did feel better when he was lying down.

The medication had relieved some of the discomfort and itching in his palms, but the prescription for his flu had no effect on his high fever. In an effort to concentrate on other things besides his mysterious affliction, Father Mancuso tried reading some of his subscription magazines, searching for articles to divert his attention from his problem. In the succeeding three hours he read through over a dozen new and old periodicals. Then he noticed a slight discoloration on the last magazine he had held.

The priest turned over his hands. The palms were smearing. The blisters looked as if they were about to burst.

By noontime George was in Syosset, working with his adding machine. He had discovered that the money that was coming in didn't balance with what was going out. The accounts payable column was becoming too one-sided lately, and he knew he would have to cut back on his field crews and office personnel.

George hated the idea of depriving men of their livelihood, particularly when he knew they'd have a hard time finding other jobs in the suffering construction industry. But it had to be done, and he wondered where to begin. George didn't dwell too long on the subject, however, because he had other pressing problems. Before the banking week was up the next day—Friday —he would again have to transfer funds from one company bank account to another to cover checks that had been issued to suppliers.

Deeply involved in these manipulations, George didn't notice the passing time. For the first moments since December 18, George Lutz was not thinking about himself or 112 Ocean Avenue.

But his wife was thinking—thinking very hard about the house. Kathy hadn't told George in so many words, but she was becoming convinced that some of the events in the past two weeks had been the work of outside forces. She was sure he would think her conclusions silly, and she had been too embarrassed to tell George of her encounter with the ceramic lion.

She now feels that she had become aware that the little bits and pieces were adding up even before George had. She was frightened and wanted to talk to someone. She thought of her mother, but quickly dismissed the idea. Joan Conners was very religious and would insist that Kathy immediately talk to her old parish priest.

Kathy wasn't quite ready to enter into a world of ghosts and demons; she wanted the discussion to remain on a more general level at first. In her heart, however, she knew perfectly well where the subject would eventually lead.

She went into the kitchen and dialed the phone number of the one person who would understand what she was looking for—Father Mancuso.

She heard the connection go through and the first ring on the other end. As Kathy waited for the second ring, she suddenly became aware that the kitchen was pervaded by a sweet odor of perfume. Her flesh crawled as she waited for the familiar touch on her body.

Father Mancuso's number rang again, but Kathy never heard it. She had hung up the telephone and run from the room.

* * *

In the Rectory, Father Mancuso had been bathing his hands in the solution and found that the bleeding in his palms had stopped. The priest had a towel in his hands when the telephone rang in his living room. He picked up his telephone after the second ring.

When he said, "Hello?" the line was disconnected. He looked at the instrument. "Well! What was that all about?" Then Father Mancuso thought of George Lutz and shook his head. "Oh, no! I'm not going through that business again!" He put down the receiver and went back into the bathroom.

The priest looked at his blisters. Disgusting, he thought. Then he looked up at his face in the mirror. "When will this end?" he said to his reflection. His illness certainly showed. The circles under his eyes were darker and there was an unhealthy pallor to his skin. Father Mancuso gingerly felt his beard. It needed a trimming, but the hand would never be steady enough to hold a pair of scissors.

Father Mancuso says that staring at his reflection in the mirror suddenly made him think of the subject of demonology. The priest was aware of the scope of the field and the various occult phenomena its study embraces. He had never liked the subject, not even when he was taking the course in his student days at the seminary, and he had never tried to become too knowledgeable.

Father Mancuso knows of other priests who have concentrated on demonology, but he's never met an exorcist. Every priest is empowered to perform the Rites of Exorcism, but the Catholic Church prefers that this dangerous ceremony be restricted to those clerics who have become specialists in dealing with obsession and possession.

Father Mancuso had kept looking into his own eyes

in the bathroom mirror, but found no answers to his dilemma. He felt it was time he confided in his friend, the Pastor of the Long Island rectory.

The morning snowfall had made traveling on the roads hazardous. As the day wore on, it got colder, and cars began to get caught in drifts and skid on icy spots all over Long Island. But the snow had stopped falling while George was driving back to Amityville from his office, and he made it home all right.

The driveway of 112 Ocean Avenue was heavy with fresh snow. George saw he would have to clear a path to the garage before moving the van into the driveway. I'll do it tomorrow, he thought, and left the vehicle parked on the street, which had been recently plowed by the city's snow trucks.

He noted that Danny and Chris had been out playing in the snow. Their sleds were parked up against the steps leading to the kitchen door. As he stepped inside, he saw that they had left a trail of melting snowy footprints through the kitchen and up the staircase. Kathy must be upstairs, he thought. If she'd seen the slush they'd tracked into her clean house, there would have been hell to pay.

George found his wife in their bedroom, lying on the bed, reading to Missy from one of the little girl's new Christmas story books. Missy was gleefully clapping her hands. "Hi gang!" he said.

His wife and daughter looked up. "Daddy!" they chorused together, leaping off the bed and encircling George with delight.

For the first time in what seemed ages to Kathy, the Lutz family had a happy supper together. Unknown to her, Danny and Chris, forewarned by George, had sneaked back down to the kitchen and wiped away all traces of their snowy entry. They sat at the table, their faces still ruddy from hours spent romping in the cold air, and wolfed down the hamburgers and french fries their mother had prepared especially for them.

Missy kept the family in smiles with her aimless chatter and the way she kept sneaking fries off the boys' plates when they weren't looking. When caught, Missy would turn her face toward her accuser and flash a mouthful of teeth, minus one, to disarm him.

Kathy felt more secure with George home. Her fears had momentarily calmed and she gave no further thought to the latest whiff of perfume earlier that afternoon. Maybe I'm getting paranoid about the whole thing, she thought to herself. She looked about the table. The warm atmosphere certainly didn't portend a visit from any more ghosts.

As for George, he had to let his depressing business operations retreat to the furthest recess of his mind. It was as though he had entered a little cocoon at 112 Ocean Avenue. This was the way he wanted life to be all the time in his new house. Whatever the world outside had to offer, the Lutzes would tough it out together from their home. He and Kathy shared a steak. Then, lighting a cigarette, George wandered off to the living room with the boys.

George had brought Harry into the house to feed him and then let him remain to rough it up with his two sons in front of the fireplace. The Lutzes had eaten early, and so it was only a little after eight when Danny and Chris began to nod.

While the boys marched upstairs to bed, followed by Missy and Kathy, George took Harry out to the doghouse. Wading through the snow that had piled up between the kitchen door and the compound, he tied Harry to the strong lead line. Harry crawled into his doghouse, turned around several times until he found his right spot, and then settled down with a little sigh. While George stood there, the dog's eyes closed and he fell asleep.

"That does it," said George. "I'm taking you to the vet on Saturday."

After putting Missy to sleep, Kathy returned to the living room. George made his usual tour of the house, now double-checking every window and door. He had already inspected the garage and boathouse doors when he took Harry outside.

"Let's see what happens tonight," he told Kathy when he came back down. "It's not blowing at all out there."

By ten P.M., both George and Kathy were feeling drowsy. His blazing fire was running out, but the heat was affecting their eyes. She waited until George had poked out the last embers and had poured water over some still-smoldering pieces of wood. Then Kathy turned off the chandelier and looked around to take her husband's hand in the darkness. She screamed.

Kathy was looking past George's shoulder at the living room windows. Staring back at her were a pair of unblinking red eyes!

At his wife's scream, George whirled around. He also saw the little beady eyes staring directly into his. He jumped for the light switch, and the eyes disappeared in the shining reflection in the glass pane.

"Hey!" George shouted. He burst through the front door into the snow outside.

The windows of the living room faced the front of the house. It didn't take George more than a second or two to get there. But there was nothing at the windows.

"Kathy!" he shouted. "Get my flashlight!" George strained his eyes to see toward the back of the house in the direction of Amityville River.

Kathy came out of the house with his light and his parka. Standing beneath the window where they had seen the eyes, they searched the fresh, unbroken snow. Then the yellow beam of the flashlight picked up a line of footprints, extending clear around the corner of the house.

No man or woman had made those tracks. The prints had been left by cloven hooves—like those of an enormous pig.

14 January 2 — When George came out of the house in the morning, the cloven-hoofed tracks were still visible in the frozen snow. The animal's footprints led right past Harry's compound and ended at the entrance to the garage. George was speechless when he saw that the door of the garage was almost torn off its metal frame.

George himself had closed and locked the heavy overhead door. To wrench it away from its frame would not only have created a great racket, but would require a strength far beyond that of any human being.

George stood in the snow, staring at the tracks and

wrecked door. His mind raced back to the morning when he had found his front door torn open and to the night he had seen the pig standing behind Missy at her window. He remembers saying out loud, "What the hell is going on around here?" as he squeezed past the twisted door into the garage.

He turned on the light and looked about. The garage was still packed with his motorcycle, the children's bicycles, an electric lawn mower that had been left by the DeFeos, the old gas-powered machine he had brought from Deer Park, garden furniture, tools, equipment, and cans of paint and oil. The concrete floor of the garage was covered with a light dusting of snow that had drifted through the partly opened door. Obviously it had been off its frame for several hours.

"Is there anybody in here?" George shouted. Only the sound of a rising wind outside the garage answered him.

By the time George drove off to his office, he was more angry than frightened. If he had any terror of the unknown, it had been dismissed by the thought of what it was going to cost him to repair the damaged door. He didn't know if the insurance company would pay him for something like this, and he just didn't need two to three hundred dollars of extra expense.

George doesn't recall how he ever maneuvered the Ford van over the dangerous snow- and ice-covered roads to Syosset. His frustration at being unable to comprehend his bad luck blocked out any concern for his own safety. At the office, he quickly occupied himself with his immediate problems and for the next several hours was able to put aside any thoughts about 112 Ocean Avenue.

Before he'd left home, George had told Kathy about

the garage door and the tracks in the snow. She had tried calling her mother, but there was no answer. Then Kathy remembered that Joan always shopped on Friday mornings rather than buck the Saturday crowds at the supermarket. She went upstairs to her bedroom, intending to change the linen in all the rooms and vacuum the rugs. Kathy's mind raced with the details of thoroughly cleaning her house for the first time. If she didn't occupy herself completely until George returned, she knew she'd fall to pieces.

She had just finished putting fresh cases on her pillows and was plumping them up when she was embraced from behind. She froze, then instinctively called out, "Danny?"

The grip around her waist tightened. It was stronger than the familiar woman's touch she had experienced in the kitchen. Kathy sensed that a man was holding her, increasing the pressure as she struggled. "Let me go, please!" she whimpered.

The pressure eased suddenly, then the hands released her waist. She felt them move up to her shoulders. Slowly her body was being turned around to face the unseen presence.

In her terror, Kathy became aware of the overwhelming stench of the same cheap perfume. Then another pair of hands gripped her wrists. Kathy says she sensed a struggle going on over possession of her body, that somehow she had been trapped between two powerful forces. Escape was impossible and she felt she was going to die. The pressure on her body became overwhelming and Kathy passed out.

When she came to, she was lying half off the bed with her head almost touching the floor. Danny had come into the room in answer to her call. Kathy knew the presences were gone. She couldn't have been out more than a moment.

"Call Daddy at his office, Danny! Hurry!"

Danny returned in a few minutes. "The man on the telephone says Daddy just left Syosset. He thinks he's coming back here."

George did not come back to the house until early afternoon. When he reached Amityville, he drove up Merrick Road toward his street and stopped off at The Witches' Brew for a beer.

The neighborhood bar was warm and empty. The juke box and television set were silent, and the only sounds in the place were those of the bartender washing glasses. When George entered, the man looked up and recognized him from the other day. "Hey, man! Good to see you again!"

George nodded in return and stood up at the bar. "A Miller's," he ordered.

George watched while the bartender filled a glass. He was a roly-poly young guy, somewhere in his late twenties, with a stomach that suggested he liked to sample the beer he sold. George took a long sip, half-emptying the tall stein before putting it down on the dark wood bar. "Tell me something," George belched. "Did you know the DeFeos?"

The young man had resumed his glass-washing. He nodded. "Yeah, I knew them. Why?"

"I'm living in their house now and . . .".

"I know," the bartender interrupted. George lifted his eyebrows in surprise. "The first time you came in here you said you just moved into 112 Ocean. That's the DeFeos'."

George finished off his beer. "They ever come in here?"

The bartender put down a clean glass and wiped his hands on a towel. "Only Ronnie did. Sometimes he brought in his sister Dawn. A cute kid." He picked up George's empty glass. "You know, you look a lot like Ronnie. The beard and all. I think you're older than he is, though."

"Did he ever talk about their house?"

The bartender put a new beer in front of George. "The house?"

"Yeah, you know, like did he ever say there was anything funny going on there? Stuff like that." George took a sip.

"You think there's something bad about the joint? I mean, now after the murders?"

"No, no." George raised a hand. "I was just asking whether he ever said anything before the, er—that night."

The bartender looked around the bar as if to confirm that there was no one else around. "Ronnie never said anything like that to me, personally." He leaned closer to George. "But I'll tell you something. I was there once. They threw a big party and Ronnie's old man hired me to take care of the bar."

George had finished half of his second beer. "What did you think of the place?"

The bartender spread his fat arms wide. "Big. A real big joint. I didn't see too much of it, though; I was down in the basement. A lotta booze and beer flowed that night. It was their anniversary." He looked around the bar again. "Did you know you got a secret room down there?"

George pretended ignorance. "No! Where?"

"Uh-hunh," the bartender said. "You take a look behind those closets and you'll find something that'll really shake you."

George leaned over the bar. "What was it?"

"A room, a little room. I found it that night I was down in the basement. There's this plywood closet built up beside the stairs. I'm using it to ice beer in, see? When I bumped a keg against one end of the closet, it seems the whole wall is loose. You know, like a secret panel, something out of an old movie."

"What about the room?" George prodded.

The bartender nodded. "Yeah, well, when I bumped the plywood, it came open, and I could see this dark space behind it. The light bulb wasn't working, so I lit a match. And sure enough, there's this weird little room, all painted red."

"You're putting me on," George protested.

The bartender put his right hand over his heart. "God's honest truth, man, so help me. You'll see."

George finished his second beer. "I'll certainly have to look for that." He put a dollar on the bar. "That's for the beers." He put down another. "That's for yourself."

"Hey, thanks, man!" The bartender looked up at George. "You want to know something really flakey about that little room? I used to have nightmares about it."

"Nightmares? Like what?"

"Oh, sometimes I'd dream that people—I don't know who they were—were killing dogs and pigs in there and using their blood for some kind of ceremony."

"Dogs and *pigs*?"

"Yeah." The bartender waved his hand in disgust. "I guess the place—the red paint and all—really got to me."

When George got home, he and Kathy both had stories to tell each other. She described the frightening event in their bedroom, and he related what the bartender at The Witches' Brew had told him about the red room in the basement. The Lutzes finally realized that there was something going on that was beyond their control. "Please call Father Mancuso," Kathy begged. "Ask him to come back."

Father Mancuso's superiors had been concerned with his health and had dropped by to look in on him. Father Mancuso told them that he felt much better that morning. They also decided to spend some time together to review the priest's workload. Most of the backlog was quickly cleared up and put in a superior's briefcase. A secretary would do the typing. Father Mancuso saw the clerics to the building's entrance and then walked back into his apartment. The phone was ringing.

He was still wearing the soft white cotton surgical gloves he had found in a drawer. The priest had explained to the Bishop that he had put them on his hands to protect them from cold, but his real motive was to hide the ugly rawness of his blisters. The priest's telephone rang five times before he picked it up. "Hello? This is Father Mancuso."

The voice on the other end came through loud and clear. "Father. This is George!"

The priest couldn't believe his ears. It was as if George was standing right in the room with him. He was so surprised that he blurted, "George?"

"George Lutz. Kathy's husband!"

"Oh! Hi! How are you?"

George held the receiver away from his ear and looked at Kathy standing next to him in the kitchen.

"What's with him?" he whispered to her. "He sounds like he doesn't remember me."

Father Mancuso knew who George was, all right, but he was still stunned to hear from him on an open line without any interference at all. "I'm sorry, George, I didn't mean to be rude. I just wasn't ready for your call this way after all the trouble I've had reaching you."

"Yeah," answered George. "I know what you mean."

Father Mancuso waited for George to continue, but there was only silence. "George? You still there?'

"Yes, Father," said George. "I'm here and Kathy's right beside me." He looked at his wife. "We want you to come back and bless the house."

Father Mancuso thought of what had befallen him the first time he had blessed the Lutzes' home. He looked at his white-gloved hands.

"Father, can you come right away?"

The priest hesitated. He didn't want to go back there, but he couldn't tell George that in so many words. "Well, George," he finally answered, "I don't know if I can right now. I have the flu again, you see, and the doctor doesn't want me running around in this cold weather—"

"Well," George interrupted. "When *can* you come?"

Father Mancuso began to look for a way out. "Why do you want me to bless the house again? You don't do that just at the drop of a hat, you know."

George was desperate. "Look, we owe you a dinner. You come, and Kathy will cook you the best steak you've ever had. Then you can stay overnight. . . ."

"Oh, I couldn't do that, George. . . ."

"Well, we'll make you drunk enough to stay!"

Father Mancuso couldn't believe what he just heard.

You just don't say such things to a priest. "Listen here, young man, you—"

"Father, we're in a lot of trouble. We need your help."

The priest's anger evaporated. "What's the matter?" he said.

"There are things happening around this house we don't understand. We've seen a lot of. . . ." The telephone line began to crackle on both ends.

"What'd you say, George. I didn't hear you."

There would be no more converstion between the two men. There was no longer anything to be heard on the line but static and a loud whirring sound. Both men knew it was no use and hung up their telephones.

George turned to Kathy and looked around the room. "It's started again. It's killed the phone."

By the time Father Mancuso put down the receiver, his hands were burning again. "God forgive me," he said aloud, "but George is going to have to get help from someone else. There's no way I'm going back to that house!"

15 **January 2 to 3** — Disappointed that they couldn't convince Father Mancuso to return to their house, George and Kathy discussed other ways of getting help. Both had agreed that now that they had already moved in, it would be unseemly to ask the local parish priest in Amityville to bless the house. Besides, he had been the confessor to the DeFeos, and George recalled from the newspaper accounts that he was an elderly man who pooh-poohed the thought of "voices" in the house telling Ronnie what to do. He wasn't much of a believer in occult phenomena.

At one point, George talked of vandalism. Possibly

someone was trying to frighten them out of the house, using violent acts of destruction to hurry their departure? Kathy had her own opinions. When she had said *something* had touched her, had George thought it was just her imagination? He didn't. Could he explain the horrible figure burned into the brick wall of the fireplace? He couldn't. Had they really seen a pig's tracks in the snow? They had. Would he agree that there was a powerful force in the house that could hurt the family? He did. What were they going to do? When they went to bed at night, George told her he had decided to go to the Amityville Police Department the next day.

During the night of January 2, George again had the urge to check out the boathouse and found Harry fast asleep in his doghouse. The next morning, he drove Harry to the animal hospital in Deer Park that he had been using and had them check the dog over thoroughly. It had cost him $35 to discover Harry was sound and didn't appear to be drugged or poisoned. The vet suggested that the animal's lassitude might possibly have developed from a change in his diet.

On the morning of January 2, Father Mancuso again blessed the Lutzes' home. He didn't perform the ceremony in Amityville, but at the church and the Long Island rectory. In the church the priest held a votive Mass—a mass that does not correspond with one prescribed for the day, but is said for a special intention, at the choice of the celebrant.

Father Mancuso had removed his gloves. He knelt at the altar and opened his missal. He began: "I am the Savior of all people, says the Lord. Whatever the troubles, I will answer their cry and I will always be their Lord."

The priest crossed himself and read aloud the opening chapter of the Mass: "God our Father, our strength in adversity, our health in weakness, our comfort in sorrow, be merciful to your people."

Father Mancuso lifted his eyes to the figure on the cross. "As you have given us the punishment we deserve, give us also new life and hope as we rest in your kindness. We ask this through Christ our Lord."

He closed his missal, but kept his eyes on Jesus. "Lord, look kindly on the Lutzes in their sufferings, and by the death of your Son, endured for us, turn away from them your anger and the punishment their sins deserve. We ask this through Christ, our Lord. Amen."

After the votive Mass, Father Mancuso returned to his apartment to find a stupefying odor of human excrement pervading his rooms!

He gagged but managed to throw open all the windows. The freezing air rushed in, providing momentary relief, but then the stench overpowered even the cold wind. Father Mancuso ran to his bathroom to see if somehow the toilet had backed up. But no, there was nothing amiss—not until you tried to breathe!

The priest knew there was a cesspool under the front lawn of the rectory and dry wells behind the parking lot. He enlisted the aid of the maintenance man and together they found that no animals had been trapped in the wells and that the cesspool was in good working order. There had been no apparent leaks in the plumbing.

Father Mancuso feared that the horrible odor might

begin to pervade the entire rectory. Other priests might be driven from their rooms to the school building across the yard. The Pastor would be extremely upset over the incident. Finally, Father Mancuso decided to burn incense to dispel the noxious stench.

Up to that point, Father Mancuso had not attributed the source of the smell to his own apartment. But after lighting the incense in his rooms and returning to the school building with the others, the priest realized that his apartment had been the first struck—evidently while he had been celebrating the special Mass for the Lutzes. He then made the terrifying connection—a disembodied voice in 112 Ocean Avenue had told him to "Get out." Whoever that voice belonged to, it had reached clear across to the Rectory to give him the same message.

There was another connection Father Mancuso had been trying to make. He realized it when he stood by the windows in the lobby and looked across to his apartment in the Rectory, remembering one of the lessons he learned in demonology—the odor of human excrement was always associated with the appearance of the Devil!

In the afternoon, Detective Sergeant Lou Zammataro of the Amityville Police Department went along with George, saw the wrecked garage door and the animal tracks still visible in the frozen snow, and then went into the house. He was introduced to Kathy and the children. She repeated her story of the ghost-like touchings and took the sergeant into the living room to show him the image burned into the fireplace wall.

Even after George and Kathy showed him the red room in the basement, they sensed Zammataro's skepticism. He had listened to George's version of the evil use of the hideaway, nodded when George mentioned Ronnie DeFeo as the builder of the secret room, then asked the Lutzes whether they had any concrete facts to base their fears on. "I can't work on what you believe you've seen or heard. Maybe you ought to get a priest in here," he suggested. "It sounds more like his kind of job than a cop's."

Sergeant Lou Zammataro left the Lutz house and got into his car. He knew he hadn't helped the young couple at all. But there was really nothing he could do for them, except maybe have a cruiser stop by once in a while. There had been no use in frightening them anymore, he had told himself as he drove off. Why make things worse by mentioning that he had felt strong vibrations, "a creepy feeling" the moment he once again walked into 112 Ocean Avenue?

When the sun went down, there still wasn't very much relief from the stench at the Long Island rectory. The heavy smoke released by the burning incense had gotten into the eyes and lungs of everyone who had entered Father Mancuso's rooms. His visitors were no longer able to tell whether they were nauseous from the smoke or from the original smell.

Father Mancuso had left his windows wide open in the hope that the cold air would eventually drive the odor from his rooms. But that effort backfired; the inrushing wind had only blocked the smoke and smell from getting out. The priest had wanted to tell the others that he knew what had happened and why, but he kept his own counsel, praying for a quick deliverance from this latest humiliation.

* * *

Immediately after Sergeant Zammataro had left, George noticed the compressor in the boathouse had stopped. There was no reason for the machine's stopping—unless it had overloaded the circuits and blown a fuse. That meant he would have to go down to the basement in the main house and examine the fuse box.

George knew the box was in the area of the storage closets and took a fresh box of fuses down with him. In the cellar he quickly discovered the blown fuse and replaced it. He heard the compressor start up again, making a loud racket as it began to churn, but waited to see if another overload would occur. After a few moments, he was satisfied and started to go back upstairs.

When he was halfway up the cellar steps, George became aware of the smell. It wasn't fuel oil.

He had his flashlight with him, but the lights in the basement were still on. From his position on the stairs, George had been able to see almost the entire cellar. He sniffed and then sensed the foul odor was coming from the area near the northeast corner—by the plywood storage closets that shielded the secret room.

George went back down the stairs and warily approached the storage closets. As he stood before the shelving that hid the small room, the odor became stronger. Holding his nose, George forced open the paneling and shone his flashlight around the red painted walls.

The stench of human excrement was heavy in the confined space. It formed a choking fog. Nauseated, George's stomach began to heave. He had just time enough to pull the panel back into place and shut out the mist before he vomited, fouling his clothes and the floor.

Father Mancuso and the Pastor of the Long Island rectory had been friends for several years, ever since the priest had taken an apartment in the rectory. Even with Father Mancuso's heavy workload and busy schedule within the diocese, their friendship had ripened and the two priests had become close companions. There was a twenty year difference in their ages, Father Mancuso being forty-two, but there was no generation gap.

On the night of January 3, all that changed. Depressed with the unrelenting, disgusting odor that permeated his apartment, Father Mancuso turned on the Pastor and their comradeship was irrevocably destroyed.

It started in the Pastor's office, where Father Mancuso had gone to pick up some reports that had been typed for him. He was about to return to his own rooms when the Pastor walked in with three other priests. Father Mancuso had just finished dinner—such as it was, since he had been unable to rid himself of the odor that clung to his clothes. He glanced across the room to the Pastor who was standing beside a desk. "I don't know why the stink is in my rooms only," he barked. "Why am I the only one chosen for this high honor?"

The Pastor was stunned. He couldn't believe what he had just heard. Why, he thought, the man's completely irrational over the incident. "I'm sorry," the Pastor said gently in reply, "but I really can't give you a logical explanation."

Father Mancuso waved his hand at the Pastor in dismissal. The other priests had looks of amazement on their faces. Father Mancuso had never spoken like this, particularly about his close friend. Now his face became red with rage. "How come you're so nice to me, eh?"

What had gotten into the man? The Pastor looked at the other priests, who were avoiding his glance, embarrassed at being included in the outbreak. Then the Pastor spoke up. "I think this business with the smell is getting the better of you, my friend. It would be better if we talked at another time and in another place." He rose to leave the room.

His determined calm deflated Father Mancuso. He retreated, but continued to glare at the Pastor. There was a look in his eyes that came from someone or something within the priest's body. This emotion had momentarily taken possession of Father Mancuso, just as something had taken possession of, and befouled, his apartment in the rectory.

George had finally managed to clean himself up after the disastrous trip to the basement. He and Kathy were sitting in the kitchen over coffee. It was eleven P.M. and both were tired from the tension of the ever-increasing incidents. Only the kitchen seemed relatively safe; and they were reluctant to go up to bed.

"Listen," George said, "it's getting chilly in here. Let's at least go into the living room where it's warmer." He got up from his chair, but Kathy remained seated.

"What are we going to do?" she asked. "Things are getting worse. I'm really scared something can happen to the kids." Kathy looked up at her husband. "God knows what's going to happen next around here."

"Look," he answered. "Just keep the kids out of the cellar until I set up a fan down there. Then I'm going to brick up the door to that room so it never bothers us again." He took Kathy's arm and pulled her up from the chair. "I also want to talk to Eric at my office. He says his girl friend's got a lot of experience investigating haunted houses . . ."

"Haunted houses?" Kathy interrupted. "Do you think this house is haunted? By what?" She followed him toward the living room, then stopped in the hall-way. "I just had a thought, George. Do you think our TM had anything to do with all this?"

George shook his head. "Nah. Nothing at all. But what I do know is that we've got to get help some-where. It might as well be. . . ."

As they entered the living room, Kathy's scream cut off the rest of George's words. He looked to where she was pointing. The ceramic lion that George had car-ried up to the sewing room was on the table next to Kathy's chair, its jaws bared at George and Kathy!

16 **January 4 to 5** — George grabbed the lion off the living room table and threw it into a garbage can outside the house. It took him quite a while to calm Kathy down because he couldn't possibly explain how the porcelain piece had managed to come back down from the sewing room. She insisted that something in the house had done it and didn't want to spend another minute in 112 Ocean Avenue.

George had confided to Kathy that he too felt uneasy about the lion's sudden reappearance. But he couldn't agree on running away without taking a chance at fighting back.

"How can you fight what you can't see?" Kathy asked. "This—this thing can do anything it wants."

"No honey," George said. "There's no way you can convince me a lot of this isn't just our imagination. I just don't believe in spooks! No way, no how, no time!" Finally he talked Kathy into going up to bed with a promise that if he couldn't get help by the next day, they would get out of the house for a while.

They both were completely drained. Kathy fell asleep out of sheer exhaustion. George dozed off, waking every once in a while to listen groggily for any unnatural noises in the house. He says that he has no idea how long he had lain there before he heard the marching music downstairs!

His head was keeping time to the drumbeats before he realized he was listening to music. Glancing at Kathy to see if she had been awakened, he heard her breathe deeply. She was fast asleep.

George ran out of the room into the hall and heard the stomp of marching feet get louder. There must be at least fifty musicians parading around on the first floor, he thought. But the moment he hit the bottom step and turned on the hall light, the sounds ceased.

George froze on the staircase, his eyes and head swiveling frantically to catch any sign of movement. There was absolutely no one there. It was as though he had walked into an echo chamber. After the cacophony of sound, the sudden silence sent chills up his back.

Then George heard heavy breathing and thought someone was right behind him. He spun about. No one was there, and he then realized he was listening to Kathy from all the way upstairs.

Fear of her being alone in the bedroom galvanized George. He raced back up the steps two at a time and into his room, turning on the light. There, floating two feet above the bed, was Kathy. She was slowly drifting away from him toward the windows!

"Kathy!" George yelled, jumping up on the bed to grab his wife. She was as stiff as a board in his hands, but her drifting stopped. George felt a resistance to his pull, then a sudden release of pressure, and he and Kathy fell heavily off the bed onto the floor. The fall awakened her.

When she saw where she was, Kathy was incoherent for a moment. "Where am I?" she cried. "What's happened?"

George started to help her up. She could hardly stand. "It's nothing," he reassured her. "You were having a dream and fell out of bed. That's all."

Kathy was still too dazed to question George any further. She said, "Oh!" meekly got back into bed, and immediately fell back into a deep sleep.

George turned out the light in the room but did not return to his wife's side. He sat on a chair beside the windows, watching Kathy and looking out at the lightening sky of early morning.

Father Mancuso was also watching the new day break—from his mother's house in Nassau, where he had gone shortly after the altercation with his Pastor. Not that he was afraid of a continued outburst, but it had been impossible to sleep in his stench-filled, incense-smoked apartment. Also, he now truly believed that he was the target of the demonic phenomenon and thought that the odor would go if he left the Rectory for a while.

At first Father Mancuso had misgivings about being in his mother's home because he didn't want to involve her in his problem. But then he had begun to feel feverish and decided that if he was to be sick again, he'd rather be under her care.

He hadn't had much sleep and awakened a few minutes before dawn. He felt his palms itching and looked at his hands to examine both sides. He considered talking to his mother, but he didn't want to upset her further; she was already deeply concerned about his illness.

The skies were laced with long streaks of white clouds. He noted they were low and moving fast. With the cold spell still holding in the low teens, that could mean more snow. Father Mancuso turned away from the window and looked at the clock on the night stand. It was only 7:00 A.M.

I'd like to call George Lutz, he thought, to find out if the Mass caused any similar reaction at his house. But no, seven might be too early. Father Mancuso decided to wait a while and got back into bed.

It was nice and warm under the covers. Sleepily he heard his mother stirring in the kitchen and suddenly he was ten years old, waiting for her to call him to get up for school. The recent pains, aches, and humiliations fled from his mind and body. Father Mancuso was sleeping safely in his old bed in his mother's house.

By ten in the morning, Kathy was still in a deep sleep. George had become worried about her condition after the past night's terrifying experience. He couldn't wait any longer. He had to call Father Mancuso again.

Danny and Chris had told their father that they heard on their radio that the Amityville schools were closed because of a heating problem. They were somewhat disappointed, because it would have been the first day at their new school after the Christmas holidays and a chance to meet some new friends.

George thought he was lucky not to have to drive the boys to school. It was clear across town, and he hadn't really wanted to leave Kathy and Missy alone in the house. He fed the children their breakfast and sent them up to play in their bedroom. Then he looked in on Kathy.

Her face was pale, drawn, with deep lines around her mouth. He didn't want to waken her and went back down to the kitchen. When he saw that it was 11:00 A.M., George decided to call the priest.

When he dialed Father Mancuso's private number, there was no answer. George called the Rectory itself and was informed that Father Mancuso was visiting his mother. No, they couldn't give out her number, but would give Father Mancuso the message that George had called.

George sat in the kitchen the rest of the morning, waiting for the return call. He thought he had been a fool to mouth off about "not believing in spooks." Kathy was right—how the hell *can* you fight something that can lift you clear off the bed like a stick of wood? George Lutz, ex-Marine, admitted he was scared.

Kathy came downstairs just as the telephone rang. It was George's office, calling to ask when he was coming in. The Internal Revenue agent was due back and they did not know how George wanted to handle the situation. George squirmed. Finally he told his bookkeeper to call their accountant and postpone the appointment until the following week. As for his coming in, he said Kathy didn't feel well and they were waiting for the doctor.

Kathy sat next to George at the kitchen table and looked strangely at her husband. She mouthed the word "doctor?" to him. George shook his head at her and ended the call by telling his office he'd get back to them later.

"Boy!" he said to Kathy, "are they ever getting fed up with me! I'll just have to go in tomorrow."

Kathy yawned at George and shrugged her shoulders in an effort to ease the stiffness in her body. "God," she said, "look at the time. Why'd you let me sleep so long? Have the kids eaten? Are the boys in school?"

George started counting on his fingers. "First," he answered, "you haven't slept so good in weeks, so I left you alone." He held up two fingers. "Yes, they ate breakfast." Three fingers: "There was no school today. I sent them upstairs to play with Missy."

Good, he thought to himself, Kathy hadn't remembered anything about what happened last night. And I'm not going to tell her. "I've been trying to get hold of Father Mancuso again," George continued. "They say he's at his mother's, but he'll call me as soon as they hear from him."

Father Mancuso's mother didn't disturb his needed rest until almost three in the afternoon. He knew his fever had dropped because he no longer had a light-headed feeling. The priest was doubly pleased when he finally checked in with the Rectory. The priest who answered the phone said that the incense had driven out the horrible smells and that Father could return to his rooms. "Father, also George Lutz called you."

Oh yes, he reminded himself, I meant to call him, but it completely slipped my mind. Father Mancuso said he'd return by evening. He then called George.

The phone was picked up on the first ring. "George? This is Father Mancuso."

"Father, am I glad you called. We must talk to you right away. Can you please come over here now?"

"But I've already blessed your house again," Father Mancuso answered. "I said a votive Mass for you at the church the other day. And by the way, did any. . . ."

"It's not to bless the house," George interrupted. "It's more than that now." For the next several minutes George recounted what had happened at 112 Ocean Avenue since he had moved in. He sent Kathy upstairs under the pretext of getting him her cigarettes, and then told the priest about her levitating. "That's why we need you, Father," George concluded. "I'm scared of what's going to happen to Kathy and the kids!"

All through George's recitation, Father Mancuso had feared a debilitating attack. Now he was ashamed to realize that he'd been avoiding the inevitable. Come on, man, he thought to himself, you're a priest. If I don't want to wear the collar and accept its responsibilities—why, by God, I'm not worthy!

Father Mancuso took a deep breath. "All right, George. I'll try and get there to . . ."

George didn't hear what Father Mancuso said next. Suddenly there were several loud moans on the line and then a crackling that almost shattered his eardrum. "Father! I can't hear you!" A continued moaning was the only answer George got.

On the other end, Father Mancuso felt as if he had been physically slapped in the face. He put down the telephone, put his hand to his cheek, and began to cry. "I'm afraid to go back there!" He looked at his sore palms and then buried his face within them. "Oh, God! Help me! Help me!"

George knew it was useless to wait for Father Mancuso to call back. Even if he did, they would have been prevented from talking to one another about the house. But George had one hope. He was sure he had heard the priest say he'd come, but he didn't know when. He'd just have to sit there and wait.

Father Mancuso returned to the Rectory after eight in the evening. Now it was almost ten o'clock, and the priest sat and stared at the telephone. The smell of excrement had gone from his quarters as he'd been told, but the acrid sting of incense still hung in the air. That he could tolerate. What he couldn't stand was his inability to go to the Lutzes. Even the thought of the children being in danger from the demonic behavior couldn't overcome his fear of what might await him at 112 Ocean Avenue.

Finally Father Mancuso decided he would call the Chancellor's office in the diocese. He picked up the telephone, but thought he would go see them in the morning instead. He then prepared to go to bed. He had had enough sleep that morning at his mother's, but he was exhausted again. Before putting on his pajamas, he went into the bathroom to remove the white gloves. The Burow's Solution had helped soothe the affliction and he wanted to soak his palms once more that night.

When he peeled off the gloves, he was stunned. He turned his hands over and examined the palms. There were no more ugly splotches or open sores. There was no sign of bleeding. The blisters were gone!

Kathy had never really come to herself all that day and night. She sat by the fireplace in the living room. George fed the children and eventually sent them off to bed. The boys didn't complain that it was too early because they knew they'd have to get up for school. Evidently the heating problem had been solved, because the local Amityville radio station had announced that the schools would be open the next morning.

George had even helped Missy take her bath. He read his daughter a story before she let him turn off her light. The last words Missy said before he closed her door were: "Good night Daddy. Good night Jodie."

When he saw it was almost eleven, George realized that Father Mancuso wasn't coming that night. Kathy had been drooping in her chair for the past hour, her eyes closing with the warmth of the fire. Finally, she announced to George she was going up to bed.

George looked at his wife. Not once had she mentioned getting away from the house. It was as though none of the frightening incidents had ever occurred and it was just natural for her to want to go to sleep. They went up to their bedroom together.

Kathy mumbled that she was too sleepy to take a bath and would do it in the morning. She was asleep as soon as her head hit the pillow. George sat on the edge of the bed for a while watching Kathy breathe deeply. Then he went out to check on Harry. The dog was asleep again, his food untouched.

George was about to reach down and shake the animal when he heard the marching band strike up in his house. He ran back in through the kitchen. The drums and horns were blasting away in the living room. George heard the stomping of many feet as he tore through the hallway.

The lights were still on, but he could see there was no one in the room. The very instant he could see into the living room, the music had cut off. George looked about wildly. "You sonsofbitches, where are you?" he screamed.

George took in great gulps of air. Then he realized there was something strange about the living room. Every piece of furniture had been moved. The rug had been rolled back. Chairs, couch, and tables had been pushed against the walls as if to make room for a lot of dancers—or a marching band!

17 January 6 — "Your story is very interesting, Frank, but if I didn't know your background as a pro, I'd honestly think you were a little nuts to believe in it." Chancellor Ryan got up from behind his desk and went to the new coffee machine across the room. Father Mancuso shook his head at Father Ryan's offer. Ryan then poured one black cup for Father Nuncio—the other Chancellor—and one for himself.

The Chancellor sat back down at his desk, sipped some of the coffee, then looked at his notes. "In your capacity as a psychotherapist, how many times have people come to you with stories like this? Hundreds, I'll bet."

Chancellor Ryan was an extremely tall man, even while sitting. He was six feet five, with a shock of white hair crowning a ruddy Irish face. The priest was well known in the diocese for his open manner in speaking to the other clerics, be they young parish priests or the Bishop himself.

Chancellor Nuncio, on the other hand, was the exact opposite; short, stumpy, black-haired, young at forty-two, while Father Ryan was well in his sixties, and with a seriousness to his approach that perfectly complemented the other Chancellor's softer touch.

The two had listened to Father Mancuso's recounting of the episodes that George Lutz had said happened at 112 Ocean Avenue, and to his own humiliating experiences, including the latest one that had just occurred at the Rectory. They were impressed with Father Mancuso's fears that the phenomena had a demonic taint to them.

Chancellor Ryan looked up from the pad on his desk and spoke to the troubled priest. "Before we offer any suggestions on how you should handle this as a participant and as a priest, Frank, I think you should know the ground rules." Father Ryan nodded to Father Nuncio.

The other priest put down his coffee. "You seem to think that there's something demonic going on in the Lutzes' house, that the place is possessed somehow. Well, let me reassure you that first of all, *places* and *things* are never possessed. Only people." Father Nuncio stopped, reached into his jacket and withdrew several short cigars. He offered them around, but the two priests declined. He lit up, puffing and talking at the same time. "The traditional viewpoint of the Church sees the devil in a number of ways: He tries through *temptation*, by which he is seen to prod men toward sin in the psychological battles with which I'm sure you're familiar."

"Oh, yes," Father Mancuso nodded. "As Father Ryan mentioned, I've seen and heard many who've come to me as a psychotherapist and as a parish priest."

Chancellor Ryan picked up the thread. "Then there are the so-called extraordinary activities of the devil in the world. Usually these are material things around a person that are affected; that might be what you're up against. We call it *infestation*. It breaks down into different categories which we'll explain in a minute."

"*Obsession*," Father Nuncio put in, "is the next step, in which the person is affected either internally or externally. And finally there is *possession*, by which the person temporarily loses control of his faculties and the devil acts in and through him."

When Father Mancuso had come to the Chancellors' office to keep his appointment, he had been somewhat embarrassed as to how to approach his problem. But he relaxed as the two priests had shown keen interest. Now with their spelling out the guidelines he must take in this kind of situation, Father Mancuso raised his hopes for deliverance from this evil.

"In investigating cases of possible diabolical interference," Chancellor Ryan went on, "we must consider the following: One, fraud and deception. Two, natural scientific causes. Three, parapsychological causes. Four, diabolical influences. And five, miracles.

"In this case, fraud and trickery don't seem plausible. George and Kathleen Lutz seem to be normal, balanced individuals. We think you are too. The possibilities therefore are reduced to psychological, parapsychological, or diabolical influences."

"We'll exclude the miraculous," Father Nuncio broke in, "because the Divine would not involve itself in the trivial and foolish."

"True," said Father Ryan. "Therefore the explanation would seem to include hallucination and autosuggestion—you know, like the invisible touches Kathy experienced—and when George thought he heard that marching band. But let's take the parapsychological line."

"Parapsychologists like Dr. Rhine, who works at Duke University in Durham, North Carolina, define four main operations in the science. The first three come under the general heading of ESP—extrasensory perception. They are mental telepathy, clairvoyance, and precognition, which could explain George's visions and 'picking up' information that seems to coincide with known facts about the DeFeos. The fourth parapsychological area is psychokinesis, where objects move by themselves. That would be the case with the Lutzes' ceramic lion—if it *did* move," he added.

Father Nuncio got up to refill his cup. "All of what we've said, Frank, is part of the suggestion we have for the Lutzes. Have them contact some investigative organization like Dr. Rhine's to come in and look at the house. They'll do extensive testing and I'm sure they can come to some conclusion short of diabolical influence."

"But what about me?" asked Father Mancuso. "What do *I* do?"

Chancellor Ryan cleared his throat and looked

kindly at the priest. "You are not to return to that house. You can call the Lutzes and tell them what we suggested. But under no circumstances are you ever to go there again."

"I thought you said I shouldn't consider a belief in such matters as this," Father Mancuso protested.

"Yes, I did," said Father Ryan. "But you've got yourself so worked up over this affair that at the moment the best thing you can do is dissociate yourself from the Lutzes and 112 Ocean Avenue."

After breakfast, Kathy dropped the boys off at their new school, then drove over to her mother's with Missy. George was alone in the house. He had gone down to the cellar to clear the odor with two fans. But when he came down the stairs, there was no trace of any of the terrible stench that had made him vomit the day before.

He sniffed but could find nothing, even when he went directly to the secret red room. George pulled the plywood paneling back open and flashed his light about the red wells. "Damn!" he said. "It couldn't have disappeared just like that. There's got to be an air hole down here somewhere."

George was searching for that possible air vent when Father Mancuso dialed his number. After the meeting, the priest had driven back to his own apartment in the rectory intending to call George with the Chancellors' recommendations. He heard the telephone ring ten times before he finally hung up. Father Mancuso thought he'd try again later when the Lutzes came home.

George was home all right, but he never heard the

telephone ring. The door to the basement was open, and usually the ringing telephone could be heard anywhere in the house.

George had no success in finding any opening where the stench could have escaped, but under the area where the front steps to the house had been constructed, he did discover something interesting. When the contractor had laid the foundation for the house at 112 Ocean Avenue, it seemed he had covered over a circular opening with a concrete lid. By squirreling around the dirt piled up against this protuberance, George accidentally loosened some of the old gravel around the base and heard it fall into water far below. He flashed his light and saw the beam hit against a wet, black shaft. "A well!" he said aloud. "That doesn't show up in the blueprints. It must have been left from the old house that was here before."

He returned to the first floor and looked at the kitchen clock. Strange, he thought, it's almost noon and I still haven't heard from Father. I'd better try him myself.

George called the Rectory. The priest picked up on the first ring. George was surprised when Father Mancuso told him he had just called and that there was no answer at the house. Then George asked Father Mancuso when he was coming, and they got down to Father Mancuso's report.

He said he'd been to see the Chancellors of his diocese and repeated their recommendation that George find an organization to conduct a scientific investigation of the house. Father Mancuso gave George the address of a Psychical Research Institute in North Carolina and suggested he get in touch with them immediately.

George agreed, but pressed the priest to come to the house.

Not until many months after he and his family had fled 112 Ocean Avenue would George Lutz learn what Father Mancuso had suffered after he originally blessed their house or of his subsequent humiliations and afflictions. Therefore, when Father Mancuso again refused to come to the house, George became confused. He said he really needed him, not some ghost-chasing outfit from somewhere down South. And who, he wanted to know, was supposed to pay for all of this? But after promising to call the parapsychologists and to let Father Mancuso know the results of the investigation, George hung up.

He was still annoyed when he called Kathy at her mother's. George told her what the priest had said, but snorted that he wasn't going to bother with anything like that. But Kathy felt they should pursue the Chancellors' recommendations telling George that he should listen to what the Church suggested.

Finally George agreed, saying he would drive to his office on his Harley chopper and type out the letter to the people at Duke. He didn't tell her he also wanted to talk to Eric, the young fellow at his office who said his girl friend was a medium.

After talking to George, Father Mancuso felt a tremendous pressure lift from his shoulders. Just the fact that he had been able to share his burden with others cleared his head completely for the first time in weeks; the responsibility he had been bearing alone had been taken away by his superiors.

The priest turned to preparing his work schedule

for the following week. It took him several hours—until dinner time—to finally nail down the program he wanted for his counseling and for his patients. He ordered Chinese food from a nearby restaurant in the vicinity and wolfed the meal while reading some clients' case histories.

George rode to his office and mailed the letter to the parapsychologists, using the Chancellors' names as his reference. He didn't really expect an immediate response to his request for an investigator, so he only put a regular stamp on the envelope instead of an airmail one. Then he telephoned Eric's girl friend, Francine.

She was terribly interested in what he had to say. Sure that she could contact whatever—or whoever—was making his and Kathy's lives miserable, she promised to come to the Lutzes' house with her boyfriend in a day or so.

Then the young woman said something that really made George's ears perk up. Out of the clear blue, she mentioned that George should look around his property for an old, abandoned, covered-up well. He didn't admit that he had already found such a place, but asked instead *why* she wanted him to do the searching.

Her answer shocked him: "I think," she said, "that your spirits may be coming from a well. You can cap it off, you know, but I bet if you do find a well under your house, there's a direct passage to it. And somehow, even if it's a tiny crack, that's all it takes. With that, 'it' can climb out when it wants to."

After thanking the girl and hanging up, George made a phone call to the Psychical Research Institute in Durham, North Carolina, and told them of the letter he had just sent. They agreed to send a field investigator as soon as possible. In turn, George agreed to pay the field man's expenses.

Father Mancuso, too, was on the telephone once more that night. The call came after eleven and was, surprisingly, from the priest who had helped him when his car fell apart on the Van Wyck Expressway.

Both clerics recalled the harrowing events of that evening and Father Mancuso asked the other priest whether he had encountered any further trouble after his windshield wipers had gone berserk. "No," his friend said. "That is, not until a few minutes ago." Father Mancuso's heart began to beat loudly against his chest.

"Frank," the other priest continued, "I just got a peculiar phone call. I don't know who it was, but he said, 'Tell the priest not to come back.'"

"What was he talking about?" Father Mancuso asked.

"I asked that. I said, 'Who are you talking about?' The voice only answered, 'The priest you helped.'"

"'The priest you helped'?"

"Yeah. I thought about that after he hung up and I couldn't remember anybody but you. Do you think he really means you, Frank?"

"He never told you who it was?"

"No. He just said, 'The priest'll know who it is.'"

"What did he actually say?"

"He said, 'Tell the priest not to come back or he'll die!'"

18 **January 6 to 7** — Earlier that day, Kathy had returned from her mother's house in time to pick up Danny and Chris at their new school in Amityville. The boys were eager to tell about their teachers, schoolmates, and playground facilities. The yard had been cleared of snow and the children had been able to enjoy some activities outside. Missy, jealous at having to stay home, kept pumping her brothers about what the girls at the elementary school were like.

The whole family ate together at six-thirty. George told Kathy what he had done about Father Mancuso's suggestion, and that he had also spoken to the girl who could contact spirits. Kathy was glad that he had called the parapsychology people instead of just waiting for an answer to his letter. But she wasn't too happy about a stranger coming into her house to talk to ghosts—particularly a young girl like Francine.

After they had finished dinner, Kathy told George she really wanted to return to her mother's until she felt the house was safe to live in. George reminded her that it was ten degrees above zero outside and snow was forecast by morning. Even though East Babylon wasn't too far up the road, he didn't think she could make it from her mother's house back to Amityville in time to get the boys to school in the morning.

Danny and Chris chimed in that they wanted to stay home—they had some homework to do, and besides, their grandmother wouldn't let them watch television after eight o'clock. Kathy finally gave in to their arguments, but felt uneasy about staying in the house another night. She told George she didn't think she could sleep a wink.

Harry had been in the kitchen with them while they were eating, and Kathy had given the dog all the scraps of meat left over from dinner. Before they went to bed, George thought that Harry might be better off staying inside that night. It was bitter cold out and would only get worse if the snow fell. Harry hadn't been served his usual dry food, and George thought the dog might be more alert after having some red meat.

While the boys did their homework, Missy took Harry up to her room to play. But Harry didn't want to stay there. He was nervous and sniveling, Kathy noted, particularly after Missy had introduced Harry to her unseen friend, Jodie. Finally the little girl had to close her door to keep Harry from running out. He crawled under her bed and remained there. Finally Chris came down for him. Harry scampered out of Missy's room and, with his tail between his legs, ran up the stairs to the third floor, where he remained the rest of the night.

At twelve, when George and Kathy finally went up to bed, she went out like a light for the third night in a row, quickly falling into a deep sleep, her breathing heavy. But George, lying on his side with his back to Kathy, was wide awake, his ears alert for any signs of the marching band.

When he first noticed the snowflakes falling outside the windows, he saw it was one o'clock on his wrist watch. The wind was rising, whipping the flakes about. Then he thought he heard a boat moving on the Amityville River. But the bedroom windows didn't face the water, and George didn't feel like getting up from his warm bed to look out from Missy's or the sewing room windows. Besides the river was frozen, so George ascribed the sound to the vagaries of the wind.

At 2 A.M. he began to yawn. His eyes were getting heavy and his body was getting stiff from lying in one position. A short while ago he had looked over his shoulder at Kathy. She was still flat on her back, her mouth open.

Suddenly George had the urge to get up and go to The Witches' Brew for a beer. He knew there were cans of brew in the refrigerator, but he kept thinking that they wouldn't shake his thirst. It had to be The Witches' Brew, and it didn't matter that it was two in the morning, or that it was freezing out. He turned to wake Kathy and tell her he was going out for a while.

In the darkness of the room, George could see Kathy wasn't in bed. He could see that she was levitating again, almost a foot above him, drifting away from him!

Instinctively George reached out, grabbed her hair, and yanked. Kathy floated back to him and then fell back onto the bed. She awoke.

George turned. He was looking at a ninety-year-old woman—the hair wild, a shocking white, the face a mass of wrinkles and ugly lines, and saliva dripping from the toothless mouth.

George was so revolted he wanted to flee from the room. Kathy's eyes, set deep in the wrinkles, were looking at him questioningly. George shuddered. It's *Kathy*, he thought, this is my wife! What the hell am I doing?

Kathy sensed the fright in her husband's face. My God, what does he see? She leaped from the bed and ran into the bathroom, flicking on the light above the mirror. Staring at her own face, she screamed.

The ancient crone George had seen was gone, her hair was upset, but it was blonde again. Her lips were not drooling any longer, nor was she wrinkled. But deep, ugly lines ran up and down her cheeks.

George, following Kathy into the bathroom, peered over her shoulder at the image. He too saw that the ninety-year-old visage had faded, but the long, black slashes still cut deeply down Kathy's face. "What's happening to my face?" Kathy yelled.

She turned to George, and he put his fingers up to Kathy's mouth. Her lips were dry and burning hot. Then he ran his fingertips gently across the deep ridges. There were three on each cheek, extending from just below her eyes down to just under the jawline. "I don't know, baby," he whispered.

George took a towel from the rack next to the sink and tried to wipe the lines away. Kathy spun about and looked into the mirror. Her scarred face stared back at her. Running her own fingers down her face, she began to cry.

Kathy's helplessness stirred George deeply, and he put his hands on her shoulders. "I'm going to call Father Mancuso right now," he said.

Kathy shook her head. "No, we mustn't involve him in this." She looked at George's face reflected in the mirror. "Something tells me he could get hurt. We'd better go and check on the kids," she said calmly.

The children were all right, but George and Kathy were unable to go back to sleep that night. They stayed in their bedroom, with the lights out, watching the snow fall. Every once in a while Kathy would hold her hands to her face, checking to feel if the ridges were still there. Finally the cold dawn broke. The snow had stopped, and there was just enough light for George to make out Kathy when she touched him on the shoulder. "George," she said, "look at my face."

He turned from his position he had taken in a chair near the window and looked at his wife. In the dawn's weak light, George could see that the lines were gone. He put his fingers up to her face and touched her skin. It was soft again, with absolutely no trace of the disfiguring scars! "They're gone, baby," he smiled gently. "They are all gone."

In spite of what Kathy had said during the night, George called Father Mancuso in the morning and caught the priest just before he went to early Mass.

George told him that he had spoken to North Carolina, where a Jerry Solfvin had promised to have an investigator come to the house immediately. Then he brought up the incident of the night before. Father Mancuso was aghast about the second levitation and the alterations of Kathy's face. "George," he said urgently, "I'm worried about what could happen next. Why don't you just get out of that house for a while?"

George assured the priest he had been thinking of doing just that, but first he wanted to see what Francine the medium had to say. Maybe she could help as she had claimed.

"A medium?" Father Mancuso asked. "What are you talking about, George? That's not a scientific investigation."

"But she said she can talk to spirits," George protested. "In fact, Father, do you know what she said yesterday? She told me there's a well hidden under my house. She's right! I found one under the stoop and she's never even been here!"

Father Mancuso became angry. "Listen!" he shouted over the phone. "You're involved in something dangerous! I don't know what is going on in your house, but you'd better get out!"

"You mean, just leave everything?"

"Yes, just go for a while," the priest persisted. "I'll talk to the Chancellors again and see if they can send someone, maybe a priest."

George was silent. He had been trying to get Father Mancuso to his house and been refused time and again. The priest's superiors had done nothing but suggest he contact some organization. Finally he had someone who sounded as if she could actually help him and Kathy. Why should he just leave everything and walk out?

"I'll tell Kathy, Father," George finally said. "Thanks." He was about to hang up.

"George, there's just one more thing," said Father Mancuso. "I seem to recall that you and Kathy were into Transcendental Meditation at one time."

"Yes, that's right."

"Do you still practice that?" the priest asked.

"No—yes. Well, we haven't really kept it up since we've moved here," George answered. "Why?"

"I was just curious, George, that's all," Father Mancuso replied. "I'm glad you're not doing it now. It might have been making you susceptible."

Right after talking with George, Father Mancuso called the Chancery in Rockville Centre. Unfortunately, Chancellors Ryan and Nuncio were unavailable and their secretary could only promise to have them call the following day. The priest was extremely agitated and prayed that things would not continue to deteriorate until the Church could bring its forces to bear against the evil that gripped 112 Ocean Avenue.

In his compassion for the Lutzes' plight, Father Mancuso forgot about his own dilemma. But in a few minutes, he was violently reminded that he too was subject to the unrelenting influence. He began to shiver and shake. His stomach heaved and his throat tightened. The priest sneezed, and his eyes watered; he sneezed again and saw blood on the tissue. Chancellor Ryan's warning, "Don't involve yourself any more!" flashed across his mind. But it was too late. Father Mancuso had all the signs of another attack of the flu!

Later that evening Eric, the young engineer who worked at George's company, arrived at the Lutzes' home with his girl friend Francine. George immediately hustled the young couple out of the bitter cold and into the living room to warm themselves in front of the big fire.

They brought an infectious cheerfulness that had been missing at 112 Ocean Avenue. George and Kathy responded and soon the four were chatting away like old friends. But under George's exterior warmth, there was an urgency. He wanted Francine to look over the house.

As he was trying to turn the conversation around to her experience with spirits, Francine beat him to it. Suddenly she got up from her seat on the couch and motioned to George. "Put your hand gently over here," she said. George bent over and waved his hand where she had pointed. "Do you feel the cold air?" Francine asked.

"Slightly," George answered.

"She's been sitting here. Now she's left. Now follow the couch. Feel it over here?"

George put his hand near a pillow. "Oh, yeah, it feels warm."

Francine beckoned George and Kathy to follow her. The three entered the dining room while Eric remained in the living room by the fireplace. Francine stood next to the big table. "There's an unusual odor here," she said. "I can't quite place it, but it's here. Whew! Do you smell *that*?"

George sniffed. "Yeah, right here. It's a smell of perspiration."

The girl headed for the kitchen, but hesitated before going into the breakfast nook. "There's an old man and an old lady. They are lost spirits. Do you smell the perfume?"

Kathy's eyes widened. Quickly she looked at George, who shrugged. "Evidently these people must have had the house at one time," Francine continued, "but they died. Only I don't think they died in the house." She turned to George and said, "I want to go to the basement now, okay?"

When George had first spoken to Francine on the telephone, he told her that mysterious things were happening in his house—but without ever really spelling out what the phenomena were, nor what had actually taken place with Kathy and himself. He hadn't discussed the touchings in the kitchen nor the smell of perfume Kathy had experienced. In any case, Francine had said she would rather draw her own conclusions after visiting the house and "talking to the spirits who live there."

Now Francine descended the stairs to the cellar. "The house is built on a burial ground or something like that," she said. She pointed to a large area of the basement where the storage closets were built. "Is that new?" she asked George.

"I don't think so," he answered. "As far as I know, it was all built at the same time."

Francine stopped in front of the closets. "There are people buried right here. Something is over them. There is an unusual odor. This should not be stuffy at all like this." She was pointing directly at the plywood paneling that hid the secret room. "Notice the chill?" Her hands were moving now, touching the wood. "Somebody was murdered, or he could even be buried under here. But this seems like a new part, like a new part has been added on, and over this grave."

Kathy wanted to run from the basement. Her husband noticed her discomfort and reached for her hand. Francine solved their dilemma. "I don't like this spot at all. It's better that we go upstairs now." Without waiting for a response, she turned and headed for the basement staircase.

As they went up to the second floor, Francine's boyfriend Eric joined them. She stood in the hallway, holding on to the banister. "I have to say that when I came up here, there was a whirling sensation. I felt a tightness on the right half of my chest."

"A pain?" Kathy asked.

Francine nodded. "Very slight, very quick. Right as you turn the corner. It disappeared quickly." She stepped to the closed door of the sewing room. "You've been having problems in here."

George and Kathy both nodded. He opened the door, half expecting to find the flies in the room. But there were none, and he and Francine walked inside. Kathy and Eric hung back in the doorway.

Suddenly Francine appeared to go into a trance. Out of her mouth came a different voice, heavier, more masculine: "I would like to make one suggestion to you. Most people find out who their spirits are and they find they like them. They don't want them to get lost or to go away. But in this case, I feel this house should be cleared or exorcised."

The voice coming from Francine began to sound familiar to George. He couldn't quite place it, but he was sure he had heard it before. "Somebody's little girl and boys . . . I see bloodstains. Somebody hurt themselves badly here. Somebody tried to kill themselves or something. . . ."

Francine came out of her trance. "I would like to go now," she announced to George and Kathy. "It's not a good time to try to talk to the spirits. I have a feeling I should go. I was born with a Venetian Veil, you know." George didn't know what she meant, but she promised George to return in a day or so—"When the vibrations are better," she explained. The couple departed almost immediately.

Back in the living room, George and Kathy were silent for a long time. Finally Kathy asked, "What do you think?"

"I don't know," George answered. "I just don't know. She was hitting things right on the head." He stood up to put out the fire. "I have to think about it for a while."

Kathy went upstairs to check on the children. Again Harry was staying with the boys since it was too cold out for even a rugged dog. George made his usual check of all the doors and locks, then turned out the lights on the first floor.

He went up the steps to his bedroom, then stopped before he reached the second floor landing. George saw that the banister above him was wrenched from its moorings, torn almost completely off the floor foundation.

At that very instant, he recalled whose voice had been speaking to him through Francine. It was Father Mancuso!

19 January 8 — On Thursday, Jimmy and his new bride Carey returned from their honeymoon in Bermuda. They called Kathy from Mrs. Conners', and Jimmy told his sister he would drop over later in the day. One of his first questions was whether she and George had found his $1,500. He was very disappointed when Kathy told him there had been no trace of the envelope.

It had taken George all morning to fit the second floor banister's broken anchor posts back in their sockets. When the boys came down for breakfast, both wanted to help, but George shooed them out of the way, telling them they had to go shopping for new shoes with their mother.

No one—Danny, Chris, Missy, or Kathy—had heard the banister being wrenched off its posts during the night. What had caused this latest damage in the house remained a mystery. George and Kathy had their own ideas, but did not voice them in front of the children.

Finally Kathy gathered herself together and herded her brood out to the van to go shopping. George took the opportunity to call Eric. He reached him at home and asked the young man if Francine had said anything after leaving their home. George was troubled to hear that the girl had been very upset with what she felt in the house. She had told Eric she didn't ever want to go back there; the presence was much too strong. She feared if she tried to talk to whatever was at the Lutzes', she would be in danger of a physical attack.

"Eric," George asked, "what's the Venetian Veil she mentioned just before you left?"

"From what Francine's told me," Eric answered, "that's a caul some babies are born with—a kind of skin covering, like a thin veil, over the face. It can be removed, but Francine says that that person is somehow blessed with a highly developed degree of clairvoyance."

George hung up and sat in the kitchen for over an hour, trying to think of where or how he could get help before it was too late.

Then the telephone rang. It was George Kekoris, a field investigator for the Psychical Research Institute in North Carolina, who said he had been told to contact George and arrange to set up some scientific tests at the Lutz home. Kekoris also said he couldn't make it that day, since he was calling from Buffalo, but would try to get there the next morning.

After speaking to Kekoris, George felt as if he had received a last-minute reprieve. Then, to pass the time until Kathy returned, he busied himself by taking down the Christmas decorations from the tree standing in the living room. Tenderly he placed the delicate ornaments on spread newspapers for Kathy to repack in cardboard boxes, taking special care of his great-grandmother's beautiful gold and silver piece.

All that Thursday morning and afternoon, Father Mancuso nursed his recurrent case of flu. He had resigned himself to his newest affliction as another show of power and displeasure by the evil force he had alienated at 112 Ocean Avenue.

This time there had been no solicitous call by the Pastor, even though Father Mancuso was sure the cleric had been informed of his new illness. He remained in his own apartment, resting in bed, using the medication he had been given on the doctor's previous visits. His fever ranged as high as 104 degrees, his stomach hurt continuously, and as the day wore on, he alternated between chills and sweating. Fortunately no marks had erupted on his palms—a sign that Father Mancuso interpreted to mean that he was receiving a lesser degree of punishment for involving himself again with the Lutzes.

Father Mancuso hadn't even attempted to reach the Chancellors' office again. The priest felt that the aches and pains would eventually lessen if he divorced himself from thinking about the Lutz situation, and so he waited for Father Ryan or Father Nuncio to get in touch with him. At one point during the afternoon, in fact, the priest hoped that the Chancellors would ignore his request for another audience. He passed the time by reading from his breviary.

By four o'clock, Kathy had returned from shopping. Since the Lutzes still had Jimmy's car, there was no way for the honeymooners to travel unless they were picked up. Kathy volunteered to go after her brother and his new wife.

George vetoed her suggestion—the icy roads to her mother's in East Babylon were still in a hazardous condition, and Jimmy's car had a stick shift—a gear system Kathy had never really mastered. George drove instead and was back in Amityville within the hour.

Kathy was delighted to see Jimmy and Carey again and spent the next hours eargerly listening to their account of every single moment they had spent in Bermuda. The newlyweds also had a bundle of Polaroid snapshots to go through with a detailed explanation behind each one. Jimmy didn't have a dime left, he said, but they had memories that would last a lifetime. Naturally they had brought some presents for the children, and that kept Danny, Chris, and Missy out of the adults' way for most of the evening.

Rather than spoil the pleasant visit by recalling their own weird experiences since the wedding, George and Kathy simply shared the excitement of the other two. Eventually Kathy and her new sister-in-law went upstairs to change the linen on Missy's bed. Jimmy and Carey would be staying overnight in Missy's room, while the little girl slept on an old couch in the dressing room down the hall.

Jimmy explained to George his plans for moving out

of his mother's house. He wanted to rent an apartment situated exactly between his mother's house and his new in-laws, who also lived in East Babylon; this way, both families would be placated for a while.

Everyone retired fairly early. Before turning in, George and Jimmy checked the house inside and out. George showed Jimmy the damaged garage door, but didn't offer any explanation beyond the theory that it was caused by a freak windstorm. Jimmy, who had been victimized of his money by an unknown source, was suspicious of something else, but he too kept silent and followed George as he checked the boathouse.

Back inside, they continued their tour of doors and windows, until both were satisfied with the security of 112 Ocean Avenue. It was eleven o'clock when the couples said goodnight to one another.

George knows that it happened at 3:15 A.M. because he had been lying awake a few minutes and had just checked his wristwatch. It was then that Carey woke up screaming.

"Oh, God, not her too!" he muttered to himself. George leaped out of bed, ran to Missy's room, and snapped on the light. The young couple were huddled together in bed, Jimmy cradling his sobbing wife.

"What's the matter?" George asked. "What's happened?"

Carey pointed to the foot of Missy's bed. "S-s-something was sitting there! It touched m-m-my foot!"

George approached the spot Carey had indicated and felt the bed with his hand. It was warm as though someone had been sitting there.

"I woke up," Carey continued, "and I could see a little boy. He looked so sick! He was trying to tell me to help him!" She began to cry hysterically.

Jimmy shook his wife gently. "Come on, Carey," he said soothingly. "You were probably having a dream, and—"

"No, Jimmy!" Carey protested. "It wasn't a dream! I saw him! He spoke to me!"

"What did he say, Carey?" George asked.

Carey's shoulders were still shaking, but gradually she looked up from her husband's cradling arms. George heard a noise behind him and a touch on his shoulder. He jumped, then looked around. It was Kathy. Her eyes were misty, as though she too had been crying. "Kathy!" Carey cried.

"What did the little boy say?" Kathy prompted her.

"He asked me where Missy and Jodie were!"

At the mention of Missy's name, Kathy bolted from the bedroom and ran to the other side of the hallway. In the dressing room the little girl was fast asleep, with one foot sticking out in the air. Kathy lifted Missy's blanket and bent her leg back under the covers, then leaned down and kissed her child on the head. George came into the room. "Is Missy all right?"

Kathy nodded.

In about fifteen minutes Carey had quieted down enough to fall asleep again. Jimmy was still nervous, but soon he too drifted off.

George and Kathy had shut the door on the couple and returned to their own bedroom. Immediately she went into the closet and took out the crucifix that hung inside. "George," she said, "let's bless the house ourselves."

They began on the third floor, in the children's playroom. In the eerie predawn silence of the cold room, George held the crucifix in front of him while Kathy intoned the Lord's Prayer. They did not go into Danny and Chris' room; Kathy said they could wait until the next day to bless that room and the ones in which Missy and Jimmy and Carey were sleeping.

They moved on to their own bedroom, and then to the sewing room on the second floor. Warning his wife to be careful of the newly repaired banister, George led the way down to the first floor, still brandishing the silver crucifix as he supposed a priest would during a holy procession.

When they completed their blessing of the kitchen and the dining room, it was just starting to get light outside. Even without turning on the lights, they could see the living room dimly visible before them. George marched around the furniture and Kathy started to recite: "Our Father who art in Heaven; hallowed be thy—"

She was interrupted by a loud humming. Kathy stopped and looked about her. George halted in midstride and looked up at the ceiling. The hum swelled into a jumble of voices that seemed to engulf them completely.

Finally Kathy clasped her hands to her ears to drown out the cacophony of noise, but George clearly heard the chorus thunder: *"Will you stop!"*

20 **January 8 to 9** — Father Mancuso felt too weak to celebrate Mass at the church, so he remained in his quarters, praying at his prie-dieu. The phone rang. It was Father Nuncio calling from the Chancellors' office to say that he and Father Ryan could see Father Mancuso.

The priest pleaded that his illness prevented him from coming to the Chancery, but asked whether he could discuss the Lutz situation over the telephone. Father Nuncio agreed and listened as Father Mancuso related the latest developments at 112 Ocean Avenue. Without hesitation, the Chancellor agreed with Father

Mancuso's suggestion that the Lutzes move out of their house for a while. Father Mancuso informed Father Nuncio of his decision not to return to the house in Amityville and said that he would merely relay the message over the telephone.

In Amityville, Kathy and George were still shaken from the previous night's performance by the unseen chorus. She had remained awake, sitting in their bedroom. George returned the crucifix to the closet wall and then he and Kathy held hands, each whispering reassuring words to soothe the other's fright. At eight o'clock, Kathy had risen from the edge of the bed and awakened the children. Jimmy and Carey came out of Missy's bedroom at eight-thirty, dressed and ready for breakfast.

After speaking to Father Nuncio, Father Mancuso called George Lutz to tell him of the Chancellors' decision. He let the telephone ring for a long time and was ready to give up when George answered. Father Mancuso assumed the instrument was up to its weird tricks, so he was surprised that he had gotten through without interference.

George said that they had just returned from seeing Jimmy off to East Babylon. Then George repeated the results of their impromptu blessing ceremony the night before. Dismayed, Father Mancuso urged George to heed the Chancellors' advice and get out of the house then and there. "And George," he said, "don't ever do that again. Your evoking God's name in the manner you did can only anger whatever is in your house. Just don't do *anything* anymore. It's already completely out of hand. . . ."

"Father," George interrupted. "What are you saying?"

The priest hesitated. Had he said too much? The Chancellors had confined any discussion of the Lutzes' case to scientific causes, and there would be a long period of investigation before the Church would acknowledge demonic influence. He hadn't meant to express his own personal fears. "I'm not sure," Father Mancuso corrected himself. "That's why I plead with you to leave your house now until some determination can be made, scientifically or . . ." The priest hesitated.

"Or what?" George asked.

"It may be more dangerous than any of us realize," Father Mancuso answered. "Look, George, many things happen that none of us can really explain away. I admit I'm very confused about what seems to be an evil force in your house. I also admit that it may be caused by more than our imaginations." The priest paused.

"George? You still there?"

"Yeah, Father. I'm listening."

"All right, then," Father Mancuso began again. "Please get out. Let things cool down for a while. If you get away, maybe we can all think this thing out with more rationality. I'll tell the Chancellors what happened last night and maybe they'll send someone right . . .'"

Father Mancuso was interrupted by Kathy's scream over the telephone. George blurted, "Call you back!" and the priest heard him bang down the receiver. He stood there in his living room, wondering what unnatural act was now being played out at 112 Ocean Avenue.

George ran up the stairs to the third floor. When he reached the landing, he saw Kathy in the hallway shrieking at Danny, Chris, and Missy.

George could see why: On every wall in the hall were green gelatinous spots, oozing down from the ceiling to the floor, settling in shimmering pools of green slime.

"Which one of you did this?" Kathy fumed. "Tell me or I'll break every bone in your bodies!"

"We didn't do it, Mama!" all three children chorused at once, dodging the slaps she was aiming at their heads.

"We didn't do it!" Danny yelled. "We saw it when we came upstairs!"

George stepped between his wife and the children. "Wait a minute, honey," he said gently, "maybe the kids *didn't* do it. Let me take a look."

He went up to one wall and stuck his finger into a green spot. He looked at the substance, smelled it, and then put a little against the tip of his tongue. "It sure looks like Jello," he said, smacking his lips, "but it doesn't have any taste at all."

Kathy was calming down after her tirade. "Could it be paint?" she asked.

George shook his head. "Nope." He tried to get the feel of the jelly by rolling it against his finger tips. "I don't know what it is, but it sure leaves a mess."

He looked up at the ceiling. "Doesn't seem to be coming from up there. . . ." George stopped. He looked around him as if realizing for the first time where he was. In a rush, he recalled the conversation he had had with Father Mancuso a few minutes before, and the dreaded word "Devil" almost slipped from his lips.

"What'd you say, George?" asked Kathy. "I didn't hear you."

He looked at his wife and children. "Nothing. I was just trying to think. . . ." He began to edge the others toward the staircase. "Listen," he said, "I'm hungry. Let's go down to the kitchen and have a bite. Then the boys and me'll come back up and clean up this gook. Okay, gang?"

Jimmy and Carey had arrived back in East Babylon. Carey was happy to be away from 112 Ocean Avenue, even if it meant being at her mother-in-law's. "I felt creepy there, Jimmy," she said, as they got out of their car. "I know I saw that little boy last night, no matter what anybody says."

Jimmy reached out and patted his wife's behind. "Aw, forget it, baby," he said. "It was just a dream. You know I don't believe in that stuff."

Carey squirmed away from Jimmy's touch, looking around to see if any neighbors were watching. But as she was about to go in the door, he grabbed her arm. "Listen, Carey," he said, drawing her close, "do me a favor. Don't mention what happened in front of Ma. She gets very upset about such things. Next thing you know, we'll have a priest over here."

Carey stood her ground. "What about our money you lost at Kathy's? You say that was a dream, too?"

Father Mancuso spent the rest of the afternoon wondering why George hadn't called him back after hearing Kathy scream. At one point, he considered calling Sergeant Gionfriddo of the Suffolk County Police to check on the Lutzes. But a policeman ringing their bell out of the blue might cause them even more alarm.

Oh, God, he thought, I hope nothing's happened. Finally the priest picked up the phone and dialed George's number.

There was no answer—because the whole family was out back in the boathouse, where the noise of the compressor drowned out the sounds of the rings. George, Danny, and Chris were dumping gobs of green jelly into the freezing water beside their boat. The compressor hose kept churning the substance, mixing it with the icy water so that it was swept below the ice.

As the boys flung it over from the narrow wooden walkway, Kathy was brushing away what fell from their pails. Missy was holding onto Harry to keep the dog out of everyone's way. George worked in silence, trying not to communicate his fears to Kathy and the children. Fortunately for him, Kathy still suspected that the children had been responsible for the mess; she hadn't yet equated the green slime with the other mysterious problems that afflicted the house.

George had been so absorbed in his thoughts that he had completely forgotten to call Father Mancuso back. By that evening, sitting beside the fireplace, Kathy was all for leaving for her mother's. But when she suggested they get out of the house that night, George suddenly went berserk. "Goddammit, no!" he shouted, jumping up from his chair, his face red with rage.

All the pressures that had been building within him finally exploded. "Every goddamn thing we own in the world is in this house!" he stormed. "I've got too much invested here to give it up just like that!"

The children, who were still up, cringed and ran to their mother's side. Even Kathy was frightened by a side of George that she had never seen. He had the look of a man possessed.

Absolutely livid, he stood at the foot of the staircase and screamed so that he could be heard in every room in the house. "You sons of bitches! Get out of my house!" Then he ran up the stairs to the third floor and into the playroom and threw all the windows open wide. "Get out! Get out in the name of God!"

George ran into the boys' bedroom, then down to the second floor and repeated his actions, shoving up each window in every room, bellowing, "Get out in the name of God!" again and again.

Some of the windows resisted his push, and he banged furiously on the frames until they loosened. Cold air poured in from outside, and soon the whole house was as frigid as the outdoors.

Finally George was finished. By the time he returned to the first floor, the anger was leaving his body. Exhausted from his efforts and panting heavily, he stood in the center of the living room, tightly clenching and unclenching his fists.

While George was on his holy errand, Kathy and the children had been rooted to a spot near the fireplace. Now they came up to him slowly, encircled him, and he lifted his arms and embraced all four frightened people.

There was a fifth, very human witness to this tableau. Sergeant Al Gionfriddo, the police officer whom Father Mancuso had wanted to call, had been making a final check of Amityville before he went off duty at nine. As he was passing down Ocean Avenue, the astonishing sight of a madman tearing around in 112, opening windows in the dead of winter, had caused him to brake his cruiser.

Gionfriddo pulled up at the intersection where South Ireland Place cuts into Ocean Avenue, directly opposite the Lutzes'. He turned off his headlights. Something was holding him back from getting out of his car and going up to that front door. He really didn't want to investigate why the owner was behaving like a lunatic. Gionfriddo sat there and watched as a woman went around and shut all the windows in the house.

That must be Mrs. Lutz, he thought. They seem to be all right now. I'll just keep my nose out of it. He sighed and turned over the motor of his car. Keeping his headlights off, the policeman slowly backed down South Ireland Place until he could make a left turn on the street that paralleled Ocean. Only then did he turn on his lights.

Over the following hour, 112 Ocean Avenue warmed up again. The heat from the radiators finally overcame the frigid air that had invaded the house, and once more the thermostat read 75 degrees.

The boys had been dozing in front of the fireplace, while Kathy held little Missy in her arms, rocking the sleeping girl. At ten o'clock she checked the children's bedrooms and decided that Danny and Chris could now go to bed.

Since his tirade, George had been completely un-communicative, silently staring at his blazing logs. Kathy left him alone, realizing her husband was trying to resolve their dilemma in his own way. After the children were tucked away upstairs, she finally went to him and gently tried to urge him out of the room.

George looked at Kathy and she saw the confusion and anger in his face. His eyes were misty; George seemed to be crying over his frustration. The poor guy deserves a break, she thought. He shook his head at her suggestion to go up to bed.

"You go," he said softly. "I'll be up in a while." His eyes returned to the dancing flames.

In her bedroom, Kathy left the lamp on George's nightstand burning. She undressed, slipped into bed, and closed her eyes. Kathy could hear the wind howling outside. The sound slowly relaxed her so that in a few minutes she began to doze off.

Suddenly Kathy sat bolt upright and looked at George's side of the bed. He still wasn't there. Then she slowly turned her head and looked behind her. She saw her image reflected in the mirrors that covered the wall from ceiling to floor, and she had the urge to get the crucifix out of the closet again.

So strong was the feeling that Kathy was halfway out of bed when she stopped and again stared into the mirrors. Her image seemed to take on a life of its own, and she could hear it saying: "Don't do it! You'll destroy everyone!"

When George came up to the bedroom, he found Kathy asleep. He adjusted the covers about his wife, then went to her nightstand and removed her Bible from its drawer. He turned out his light and silently left the room.

George returned to his chair in the living room, opened the Bible and began at the beginning, the Book of Genesis. In this first book of God's revelations, he came upon verses that caused him to reflect upon his predicament. He read one aloud to himself: "And the Lord God said to the serpent: Because thou hast done this thing, thou art cursed among all cattle, and beasts of the earth: upon thy breast shalt thou go, and earth thou shalt eat all the days of thy life."

George shivered. The serpent is the Devil, he thought. Then he felt a hot blast on his face, and he snapped his head up from the book. The flames of the fireplace were reaching out for him!

George leaped off his chair and jumped back. The fire he had left to die was roaring to life again, the blaze filling the entire hearth. He could feel its searing heat. But then he was stabbed in the back by an icy finger.

George whirled about. Nothing was there, but he could feel a draft. He could almost see it in the form of a cold mist coming down the staircase in the hallway!

Gripping the Bible tightly, George raced up the steps toward his bedroom. The cold wrapped itself about him as he ran. He stopped in his bedroom doorway. The room was warm. Again he was struck by the icy fingers.

George ran to Missy's bedroom and flung open the door. The windows were wide open, the below-freezing air pouring in.

George grabbed up his daughter from her bed. He could feel her little body was icy and shivering. Rushing out of the room, he ran back to his bedroom and put Missy under the cover. Kathy woke up. "Warm her up!" George yelled. "She's freezing to death!"

Without hesitation, Kathy covered the little girl with her own body. George ran out of the room and up to the third floor.

The windows in Danny and Chris' bedroom, George found, were also wide open. The boys were asleep but burrowed completely under their blankets. He gathered both in his arms and staggered down the stairs to his bedroom.

Danny's and Chris' teeth were chattering from the

cold. George pushed them onto the bed and got under the blankets with them, his body on top of theirs.

All five Lutzes were in one bed, the three children slowly thawing out, the two parents rubbing their hands and feet. It took almost a half hour before the children's body temperatures seemed back to normal. Only then did George realize he was still holding onto the Bible. Knowing he had been more than warned, he flung it to the floor.

21 January 10 — On Saturday morning, Kathy's
mother, Joan, received a frantic call from her daughter:
"Ma, I need you immediately." When Mrs. Conners
tried to question Kathy over the phone as to what had
happened she said only that there was no way to explain; her mother had to see for herself. The older
woman took a cab from East Babylon to the house in
Amityville.

George let his mother-in-law in and hurried her upstairs to Kathy's bedroom. Coming back down, he
cautioned Danny, Chris, and Missy to finish their
breakfast. When he left the kitchen to join the two

women upstairs, the children were unnaturally subdued and meekly obeyed their father. But judging from the way they were eating, they had evidently recovered from their freezing experience the night before.

When George entered his bedroom, his mother-in-law was examining Kathy, who lay on the bed naked beneath her open bathrobe. Kathy watched as her mother's finger traced the ugly welts that extended from just above her pubic hairline to the bottom of her breasts. The streaks were flaming red as though she had been burned by a hot poker slashed laterally across Kathy's body.

"Ow!" her mother winced, jerking a finger back from one of the welts on Kathy's stomach. "I burned myself!"

"I told you to be careful, Mama!" Kathy cried. "It happened to George, too!"

Kathy's mother looked at him, and George nodded. "I tried putting some cold cream on them," he said, "but even that didn't help. The only way you can touch her is with gloves."

"Did you call the doctor?"

"No, Ma," Kathy answered.

"She didn't want the doctor," George broke in. "She only wanted you."

"Does it hurt, Kathy?"

The frightened girl began to cry. George answered for her. "They don't seem to. Only when she touches them."

Kathy's mother put a hand to her sobbing girl's hair, stroking it gently. "My poor baby," she said. "Don't you worry now, I'm here. Everything's going to be all right." She leaned forward and kissed Kathy's tear-stained face. Then she closed Kathy's bathrobe, softly folding it over her inflamed body. She stood up. "I'm going to call Dr. Aiello."

"No!" cried Kathy. She looked at her husband, her eyes wild. "George!"

George put his hand out to Mrs. Conners. "What are you going to tell him?"

Kathy's mother was confused. "What do you mean?" she asked. "You can see she's burned all over her body."

George was insistent. "But how are you going to explain it to him, Ma? We don't even know how it happened. She just woke up that way. He'll think we're nuts!"

He hesitated. If he told Kathy's mother any more about what had happened during the night, he would have to disclose the demonic events that were plaguing the house. Knowing Mrs. Conners' heavily Church-oriented background, George felt sure that she would insist upon Kathy and the children leaving until she could talk to her priest. George had met the cleric and knew him to be very much like the elderly confessor at St. Martin of Tours in Amityville—unworldly when it came to anything beyond simple parish duties. In reality, George would have welcomed a priest, but not the one from East Babylon. And he did expect to hear momentarily from George Kekoris, the psychical investigator.

"Let her rest a while, Ma," he finally said. "The marks seem to be easing up from what they were before. Maybe they'll go away soon." He was remembering the slash lines on Kathy's face.

"Yeah, Mama," Kathy said, also fearing to involve her mother any more deeply. "I'll lie here a little longer. Can you stay with me?"

Kathy's mother looked from her daughter to George. There's something going on that they're not telling me about, she thought to herself. She would have liked to tell Kathy that she had never liked this house; that each time she was here she felt uncomfortable. She just did not trust 112 Ocean Avenue. Looking back, Mrs. Joan Conners now knows why.

George left the two women upstairs and went down to the kitchen. Danny, Chris, and Missy had finished their food and had even cleared off the table in the breakfast nook. When he came in, there were questions in their eyes. "Mama's all right," George assured them. "Grandma's going to stay with her."

He put his hand on top of Missy's head and turned her toward the doorway. "Come on, gang," George said, "let's go out for a while. We gotta get some things at the store, and I want to stop at the library."

After George and the children had driven off, Kathy's mother left her daughter alone for a few minutes and went downstairs to the kitchen to call Jimmy. Her son would want to know why she had rushed off to Kathy's so hurriedly. Jimmy had wanted to drive Mrs. Conners to Kathy's but she said he should stay at home in case she needed anything from her house.

Over the phone, she told Jimmy that Kathy only had some stomach cramps; she'd call him later when she was about to leave. Jimmy didn't believe her and said he wanted to come over with Carey. He was *not* to come, his mother yelled at him, and he wasn't to bring Carey. She didn't want the report that Jimmy's family was a little crazy to get back to her son's new in-laws.

Kathy, lying in bed, could hear her mother downstairs, shouting into the telephone at her brother. She sighed and opened her robe once more to look at the burning red marks on her body. The welts were still there, but they did seem fainter. Then she tried touching one of the slashes under her right breast. Her finger rested on the ugly spot. It seemed to Kathy that the sensation wasn't as severe as before. The reaction was more like putting her finger under very warm water. Again she sighed.

Kathy was about to close her bathrobe when she sensed someone was staring at her nakedness. The feeling of a presence came from right behind her, but Kathy couldn't bring herself to turn and look. She knew the mirrored wall was there and she was afraid that in it, she would see something terrible. Paralyzed with fear, she was unable to even raise her arms to draw the robe about her. She remained that way, her body completely exposed, her eyes tightly shut, cringing inwardly, waiting for the unknown touch.

"Kathy! What are you doing! You'll catch your death of cold!" It was her mother, back from the kitchen.

Even after the red welts had completely disappeared, Mrs. Conners didn't want to leave Kathy. When George returned with the children, she argued that the whole family\should leave 112 Ocean Avenue. *He* could stay if he wanted, but she insisted her Kathy and her grandchildren go.

By then, Kathy was asleep upstairs and after the latest episode, George didn't want to awaken her. "Let her sleep a little longer, Ma," he said. "We'll see about coming over later."

His mother-in-law had agreed reluctantly, getting him to promise to call her the minute her daughter awoke. "If you don't, George, I'll be back!" She warned him. He called her a cab, and she returned to East Babylon at four in the afternoon.

At the Amityville library, George had been able to secure a temporary borrower's card and take out one book—on witches and demons. Now that his mother-in-law had gone home, he sat alone in the living room, deep in the subject of the Devil and his works.

It was after eight in the evening before George finished his borrowed book. During the afternoon, Kathy's mother had prepared spaghetti and meatballs that George set out at suppertime. Danny, Chris and Missy ate while George continued reading. The last time he had looked in on Kathy, she stirred a little and he thought she was about ready to awaken from her much needed rest. Now he was in the kitchen and the three children were in the living room watching television.

George had made notes while going through the book, and now he looked at what he had jotted down. On the pad was a list of demons, with names he had never heard of. George tried to pronounce them aloud, and they rolled strangely off his tongue. Then he decided to call Father Mancuso.

The priest was surprised that the Lutzes were still at 112 Ocean Avenue. "I thought you were going to leave the house," he said. "I told you what the Chancellors said to do."

"I know, Father, I know," answered George. "But now I think I know how to lick this thing." He picked up the book from the table. "I've been reading about how these witches and demons work. . . ."

Good Lord, Father Mancuso thought, I'm dealing with a child, an innocent. Here the man's house is about to explode under him and his family, and he's talking to me about witches. . . .

". . . And it says here if you hold an incantation and repeat those demons' names three times, you can call them up," George went on. "There's a ceremony in here that shows you exactly what to do. Iscaron, Madeste!", George began to chant. "Those are the names of the demons, Father. . . ."

"I know who they are!" Father Mancuso blurted.

"Then there's Isabo! Erz, erz—this one's hard to pronounce. Erzelaide. She has something to do with voodoo. And Eslender!"

"George!" the priest cried. "For God's sake! Don't invoke those names again! Not now! Not ever!"

"Why, Father?" George protested. "It's right here in this book. What's wrong with. . . ."

The telephone went dead in George's hand. There was an unearthly moan, a loud clicking, and then just the sound of a disconnected line. Did Father Mancuso hang up on me? George wondered. And what's happened to this guy Kekoris?

"Was that my mother?"

George turned and saw Kathy standing in the doorway. No longer in her bathrobe, she had combed her hair and was wearing slacks and a sweater. Her face was slightly flushed.

George shook his head. "How do you feel, honey?" he asked. "Have a good sleep?"

Kathy lifted up her sweater, baring her navel. "It's gone." She stroked herself. "They're not there anymore." She sat down at the table. "Where are the kids?"

"They're watching television," George answered. He took her hands in his. "You want to call your mother now?"

Kathy nodded. She felt strangely relaxed, almost

sensual. Ever since she had the sensation of being stared at in her bed, Kathy had been in a languorous mood, as if she had been completely satisfied sexually. It had even carried over into her recent nap, she mused, when she had unconnected visions of making love to someone. It wasn't George. . . .

Kathy dialed her mother's number while George went into the living room with the children. He heard a loud clap of thunder. Looking out the windows, he saw the first raindrops strike the panes. Then somewhere in the distance, a flash of lightning hit the darkness and again, a few moments later, came another boom of thunder. George could make out the silhouettes of trees swaying in the rising gusts.

Kathy came into the room. "My mother says it's raining cats and dogs there," she announced. "She wants us to use our van rather than have Jimmy come for us."

The rain was coming down much harder now, beating heavily against the windows and outside walls. "From the sound of that," George said, "none of us is going anywhere at the moment."

When she had left her bedroom, Kathy opened the windows about an inch to air out the room. Even if there wasn't much room for water to get in, with the coming storm, she wanted to play it safe. "Danny," she called. "Run up to my room and close the windows tight. Okay?"

George himself ran out to bring Harry inside. In spite of the sheets of icy rain that lashed at him, George could feel the cold spell was breaking up. The rains would wash away the dirty piles of accumulated snow. There was a problem living right on the river though, for such a heavy rainfall could add to the frozen waters and overflow the bulkheads.

George came back inside, with Harry gratefully shaking himself, just in time to hear Danny, still upstairs, cry out in pain. Kathy raced ahead of George up the stairs to their bedroom. Danny stood at a window, the fingers of his right hand trapped under the window. With his left he was trying to push up the heavy wooden frame.

George pushed Kathy aside and ran to the boy who was yelling and trying to pull his fingers free. George tried to slide the window back up, but it refused to budge. He hammered at the frame but instead of releasing itself, the window vibrated, only hurting Danny more. In his frustration, George became furious and started to curse, shouting obscenities at his unseen, unknown enemies.

Suddenly the window came free on its own and shot up a few inches, freeing Danny. He grabbed his fingers in his other hand, cradling them and crying hysterically for his mother.

Kathy took the injured hand in her own. Danny didn't want to open his fist, and she had to shout at him. "Let me *see*, Danny! Open your fist!"

Averting his eyes, the boy extended his arm. Kathy screamed when she saw what his fingers looked like— all except the thumb were strangely flat. Even more frightened by his mother's anguished cry, Danny jerked his hand away.

George exploded. Running like a madman again from room to room, he screamed invectives, challenging whatever was doing this to his family to come out and fight. There was as much of a storm raging inside

112 Ocean Avenue as outside, as Kathy chased after her husband asking him to call a doctor for Danny.

The rage within George soon spent itself. He suddenly became aware that his little boy was hurt and needed medical attention. He ran to the kitchen telephone and tried to call Kathy's family doctor, John Aiello. But the line was dead. As he later learned, the storm had torn down a telephone pole, locking the Lutzes in their house even more effectively.

"I'll have to drive Danny to the hospital," George shouted. "Put his jacket on!"

The Brunswick Hospital Center is on Broadway in Amityville, no more than a mile from the Lutzes' house. Because of the hurricane-force winds raging through Long Island's South Shore, it took George almost fifteen minutes to get there.

The intern on duty was amazed at the condition of Danny's fingers, which were flattened from the cuticle to the second knuckle. But though they certainly looked crushed beyond repair, they were not broken, with no smashed bones or cartilage. He bandaged them securely, gave George some children's aspirin for Danny and suggested they return home. There was nothing more he could do.

By then, the young boy was more frightened from the way his fingers looked than from any pain. While George drove home, he held his hand stiffly against his chest, sobbing and moaning. Again it took George close to twenty minutes to drive back to 112 Ocean Avenue. The winds whipped the front door of the house back against the building, and he had trouble trying to close it behind him.

Kathy had put Chris and Missy in her own bed and was waiting in the living room. She picked up her eldest and rocked him in her arms. Danny finally cried himself to sleep, exhausted by the gruelling pain and fear.

George carried Danny up to their bedroom. Taking off only the boy's shoes, he slid him under the covers next to the other two children. Then he and Kathy sat down in chairs by the windows and watched the rain smash against the panes.

They dozed fitfully all the rest of the night. They had to stay home—it was impossible to try and get to Kathy's mother or to any other place to sleep—but they were alert to any other dangers that might threaten their children or themselves. Toward dawn both fell asleep.

At six-thirty George was awakened by the rain spattering against his face. For an instant he thought he was outdoors—but no, he was still inside in his chair by the window. Jumping up, he saw that every window in the room was wide open, some frames torn away from their jambs. Then he heard the wind and rain coming through in other parts of the house. He rushed out of the bedroom.

Every room he went into was in the same condition —window panes broken, the doors on the second and third floors smashed open—even though every one had been locked and bolted! All the Lutzes had slept through what must have been a terrible racket.

22 January 11 — The Lutzes had lived at 112
Ocean Avenue for twenty-five days. That Sunday was
one of the worst.

In the morning, they discovered that the battering
rain and wind of the night before had left the house a
complete mess. Rainwater had stained the walls, curtains, furniture, and rugs, from the first floor to the
third floor. Ten of the windows had broken panes and
several had their locks bent completely out of shape,
making it impossible to shut them tightly. The locks
to the doors of the sewing room and playroom were
twisted and forced out of their metal frames; these
couldn't be closed at all. If the family had any intention of leaving for safer quarters, that idea had to be
shelved in order to get the house back in shape and
secured.

In the kitchen, some of the cabinets were soaked and

warped. Paint was chipped on the corners of almost every cabinet. Kathy hadn't really thought about those problems yet; she had her hands full mopping up almost an inch of muddy water that had accumulated on her tile flooring. She hoped she could dry the floor before the tiles peeled loose from their cement backing.

Danny and Chris had two large rolls of paper towels and were going from room to room wiping down the walls. When they had to reach beyond their arms' length, they used a little kitchen stepladder. Missy trailed along with the boys, picking up the wet towels they discarded and throwing them into a large plastic garbage bag.

George took down every set of curtains and drapes in the house. Some could be machine-washed, and those he carried downstairs to the basement laundry. The others that would have to be dry-cleaned were put in a pile in the dining room, the driest room in the house.

The Lutzes were strangely silent while they worked that morning and afternoon. This newest disaster had only made them more determined to survive in 112 Ocean Avenue. Nobody said it, but George, Kathy, Danny, Chris, and Missy Lutz were now ready to battle any force, natural or unnatural.

Even Harry was putting on a show of toughness. The half-breed malamute was on his lead in his compound, stalking back and forth through the mud, his tail high, teeth bared. The growls and snarls that came from deep within his heavy chest were signs that the dog would tear to shreds the first person or thing he didn't recognize. Every once in a while, Harry would stop his pacing, stare at the boathouse and let out a wolf-like howl that sent shivers down the spine of everyone who lived on Ocean Avenue.

When George finished with the sodden curtains, he began to work on the windows. First he cut heavy plastic sheets to cover the broken panes and sealed them to the window frames with white adhesive tape. It wasn't a pretty sight from the inside or out, but at least it kept out the steadily falling drizzle.

George had guessed right. The temperature had risen with the storm, and it was above freezing. A lot of damage had been done to the trees and bushes along Ocean Avenue, and looking up South Ireland Place, George could see that it too had its share of broken branches lying in the street. He did note, however, that the neighbors on either side of his house had no broken windows or any other exterior damages. Only me, George thought. Terrific!

The locks on the windows and doors were a more difficult matter. George didn't have the hardware to replace the catches on the windows, so he used a pair of pliers to twist off the smashed pieces of metal. Then he hammered heavy nails into the edges of the wooden frames and challenged his unseen foes: "Let me see you pull those out, you sons of bitches!"

The locks to the sewing room and playroom doors he removed completely. In the cellar he found some one-inch pine boards that were perfect for his needs. The doors opened outward into the hallway, so George nailed the boards diagonally across both. For whatever might have remained in the two mysterious rooms, there was no longer a way out.

George Kekoris finally telephoned, saying he'd like to come out and spend a night. There was only one problem—since Kekoris had no equipment with him, the Psychical Research Institute would have to consider

the visit an informal one. He would have to draw conclusions without the rigorous controls required for
scientific evaluation.

George said that didn't matter; he just wanted confir-
mation that all the weird events in their house weren't
the product of his or Kathy's imagination. Kekoris asked
George whether any sensitives had been there, but
George didn't understand what he meant by that term.
The field investigator said they would go into that when
he came to visit.

Before George hung up, Kekoris asked whether there
was a dog in the house. George said he had Harry, a
trained watch dog. Kekoris said that was good because
animals were very sensitive to psychic phenomena.
Again George was puzzled—but at least he had the first
tangible evidence that help was on the way.

At three in the afternoon, Father Ryan left the Chancery in Rockville Centre. The Chancellor was concerned about Father Mancuso's mental welfare in the
Lutz case, and since one of his duties in the diocese
was to minister to the rectories, Father Ryan decided
that now would be a good time to visit the Long Island
rectory.

He found the bearded priest recovering from his
third attack of flu in the past three weeks. Father Ryan
said he was well aware of how highly the Bishop es-
teemed Father Mancuso as a cleric. But he wanted to
know if Father Mancuso thought the recurring affliction could be psychosomatic. Wasn't it possible that
his emotional state could be influencing his rash of
illnesses?

Father Mancuso protested that he was rational, that
he still believed that strong evil forces were responsible

for his debilitation. He was willing to undergo a psychiatric examination by anyone the Chancellors selected.

The Chancellor made no further demand that Father Mancuso remain away from 112 Ocean Avenue, but stated that the decision would have to be his.

Father Mancuso was surprised and frightened. He understood he was being tested: If he did accept responsibility for the Lutzes, he would have the Chancellors' approbation; and if not, they would understand. But there was no way he was going to involve himself to that extent. He was deeply moved by the anxiety and problems that the Lutzes were undergoing and he could not, in conscience as a priest, simply excuse his own inherent fear, but he *was* terrified.

Father Mancuso finally said that before he made any more decisions in the case, for the Lutzes and for himself, he would like to talk directly to the Bishop. Chancellor Ryan recognized the urgency in the priest's request and said he would be in touch with the superior later in the day. He would call Father Mancuso that evening.

Kathy's mother called her around six o'clock, wanting to know if they were coming to her house to spend the night. Kathy took it on herself to say no: the house was still a mess after the storm and she would have a lot of washing to do the next morning. And besides, Danny and Chris would have school, and they were missing too many days as it was.

Mrs. Conners reluctantly agreed, but made Kathy promise that she would call if anything out of the ordinary occurred; her mother would then send Jimmy over immediately. After Kathy hung up, she wondered aloud to George if she had done the right thing.

"We're gonna stick it out," he said. "Before you send the kids to bed, I'm going to go through the whole house with Harry. Kekoris said dogs are very sensitive to things like this."

"Are you sure you won't make them mad again?" Kathy asked. "You know what happened when we went around with the crucifix."

"No, no, Kathy, this is different. I just want to see if Harry can smell or hear anything."

"And what if he does? What are you going to do then?"

The dog, still in his aggressive mood, had to be kept on his leash. Harry was very powerful and George had to take a snug grip just to keep from being pulled along. "Come on, boy," he said, "sniff me out something." They went down to the basement.

George removed the leash from Harry's collar and the dog leaped forward. He circled the cellar, sniffing, sometimes scratching at spots along the bottom of the walls. When the dog came up against the storage closet that hid the red room, Harry again sniffed at the base of the paneling. Then his tail dipped between his legs, and he sank to his haunches. Harry began to whimper, turning his head to George.

"What is it, Harry?" George asked. "You smell something there?" Harry's whimpers grew more frantic and he began to crawl backwards. Then he barked at George, stood up, and ran back up the cellar steps. He waited at the top, quivering, until George came up and opened the door for him.

"What happened?" Kathy asked.

"Harry's afraid to go near the secret hideaway," George told her. He didn't put on the leash again, but walked Harry through the kitchen, dining room, living room, and enclosed porch. The dog's spirits picked up and he friskily sniffed around each room. But when George tried to take him upstairs, Harry hung back on the first step of the staircase.

"Come on," George urged him. "What's the matter with you?" The dog put one paw on the next step, but wouldn't move beyond that.

"I can get him upstairs!" Danny shouted. "He'll follow me!" The boy climbed past the dog and beckoned to him.

"No, Danny," George said. "You stay here. I'll handle Harry." George reached down and jerked the dog's collar. Harry moved reluctantly, then ran up the steps.

The dog walked around freely in both the master bedroom and the dressing room. Only when he approached Missy's room did Harry hang back. George put both hands on the dog's haunches and pushed him, but he wouldn't enter her room. Harry behaved the same way in front of the boarded-up sewing room. Whimpering and whining with fear, Harry tried to wedge himself behind George.

"Goddammit, Harry," he said, "there isn't anyone in there. What's bugging you?"

As soon as Harry came into the boys' room on the third floor, he jumped up on Chris' bed. George chased him off. Shooed out of the room, the dog headed directly for the stairs, passing the play room without so much as a glance. George couldn't catch up with him.

George arrived downstairs behind the dog. "What happened?" Kathy asked.

"*Nothing* happened, that's what happened," he said.

* * *

Father Mancuso confirmed his appointment with the Bishop's secretary. The prelate personally telephoned and suggested that if the priest felt well enough to travel, he should be at the Rockville Centre diocese the following morning.

Father Mancuso said that it was only fifteen minutes away, and his temperature was normal. Though high winds were forecast, the weather promised to remain above freezing. Father Mancuso told the Bishop's secretary that all signs pointed to his being there.

At the Lutzes', as the day came to a close, the whole family was again in the master bedroom. The three children were in the bed, and George and Kathy were sitting up in chairs next to the damaged windows. The room seemed overly warm and everyone's eyes had begun to sting. George and Kathy thought it was from fatigue. One after another, they drifted off—first Missy, then Chris, Danny, Kathy, and finally George. Within ten minutes, everyone was fast asleep.

But very shortly, George was rudely shoved awake by his wife. She and the children were standing in front of his chair, tears in their eyes. "What's the matter?" he mumbled sleepily.

"You were screaming, George," Kathy said, "and we couldn't wake you up!"

"Yeah, Daddy!" cried Missy. "You made Mama cry!"

Not fully awake, feeling almost drugged, George was completely befuddled. "Did I hurt you, Kathy?"

"Oh, no, honey!" she protested. "You didn't touch me."

"What happened, then?"

"You kept yelling, 'I'm coming apart!' And we couldn't wake you up!"

23 January 12 — George couldn't understand. Why did Kathy say he was yelling, "I'm coming apart!"? He knew perfectly well what he had said was "I'm coming *unglued*."

Now he remembered he had been sitting in the chair when suddenly he felt a powerful grip lift up the chair with him in it and slowly turn him around. Powerless to move, George saw the hooded figure he had first seen in the living room fireplace, its blasted half-face glaring at him. The horribly disfigured features became clearer to George. "God help me!" he screamed. Then he saw his own face emerge from beneath the white hood. It was torn in two. "I'm coming unglued!" George yelled.

Now still groggy, he began to argue with Kathy. "I know what I said," he muttered. "Don't tell me what I said!"

The others backed off. He's still asleep, Kathy thought, and he's having a bad dream. "You're right, George," she said gently. "You didn't say that at all." She pulled his head to her breast.

"Daddy," Missy broke in, "come to my room. Jodie says he wants to talk to you!"

The urgency of his daughter's voice broke the spell. George snapped out of it and jumped up, almost bowling Kathy over. "Jodie? Who's Jodie?"

"That's her friend," answered Kathy. "You know— I told you she makes up imaginary people. You can't see Jodie."

"Oh, yes, Mama," Missy protested. "I see him all the time. He's the biggest pig you ever saw." Then she trotted out of the room and was gone.

George and Kathy looked at each other. "A pig?" he said. It struck them both at the same time. "The pig's in her room!" George ran after Missy. "You stay here!" he yelled at Kathy and the boys.

Missy was just climbing on the bed when George stopped outside her bedroom door. He didn't see Jodie or anything like a pig. "Where's this Jodie?" he asked Missy.

"He'll be right back," the little girl said, settling the covers around herself. "He had to go outside for a minute."

George let out his breath. After the weird dream of the hooded figure, George had expected the worst when he heard the word "pig." His neck felt stiff and he rotated it, trying to work out the tight feeling. "It's all right!" he yelled back to Kathy. "Jodie's not here!"

"There he is, Daddy!"

George looked down at Missy. She was pointing to one of her windows. His eyes followed her finger and he started. Staring at him through one of the panes were two fiery red eyes! No face, just the mean, little eyes of a pig!

"That's Jodie!" cried Missy. "He wants to come in!"

Something rushed past George on his left. It was Kathy, screaming in an unearthly voice. In the same move that it took her to reach the window, she picked up one of Missy's little play chairs and swung it at the pair of eyes. Her blow shattered the window and shards of glass flew back on top of her.

There was an animal cry of pain, a loud squealing— and the eyes were gone!

George rushed to what was left of the second-story window and looked out. He saw nothing below, but he still heard the squealing. It sounded as if it was headed for the boathouse. Then Kathy's crying whimper caught George's attention. He turned to his wife.

Kathy's face was terrifying. Her eyes were wild and her mouth was tightly screwed up. She was trying to choke out words. Finally she blurted: "It's been here all the time! I wanted to kill it! I wanted to kill it!" Then her whole body slumped.

George caught his wife and silently picked her up. He carried Kathy into their bedroom, Danny and Chris following. Only Chris saw his little sister get out of bed, go to the smashed window, and wave. Missy turned away only when George called her to come into his bedroom.

* * *

In the morning, while George and Kathy were still dozing in their chairs, the children asleep in the big bed, Father Mancuso bundled up and drove to Rockville Centre.

He shivered in the cold, nippy air. Father Mancuso hadn't been outside too often since winter started and after the ride he felt a little giddy. He was grateful when the Bishop's secretary offered him tea. The young priest had often spoken with Father Mancuso and he admired the older priest's legalistic mind. They chatted until the Bishop buzzed.

The meeting was brief—all too short for what Father Mancuso had in mind. The prelate, a venerable, white-haired cleric, was a moralist of national reputation. He had the Chancellors' file on the Lutz case on his desk, but to Father Mancuso's surprise, he viewed the report with reluctance and caution.

The Bishop was very firm about the priest's dissociating himself from the Lutzes and said he'd already assigned another cleric to pick up the investigation.

Father Mancuso had nothing to say. "Possibly you should see a psychiatrist," the Bishop continued.

At that, Father Mancuso became upset. "I will if I may choose my own."

The Bishop read the displeasure in his visitor's manner, and his voice softened. "Look, Frank," he said, "I'm doing this for your benefit. You've become obsessed with the idea that demonic influence is involved. I get the impression that a good deal of it centers around you personally. That may or may not be."

Standing up, the Bishop walked around his desk to Father Mancuso's chair and put his hand on the priest's shoulder.

"Let someone else pick up the burden," he said. "It's

affecting your health. I've got too much for you to do here. I don't want to lose you. You do understand, Father?"

On Monday morning, Kathy was determined that Danny and Chris go to school. Ready to fly apart herself, she stiffened her backbone and did her duty as a mother. While George slept on, she awakened the boys, fed them breakfast, and took all three children with her in the van.

George was up when she returned with Missy. As she had coffee with him, Kathy realized he was still in a zombie-like state after the previous night's affair. For the moment, Kathy was determined to be strong for both of them. She talked to her husband in everyday terms, slipping in the reminder that he had to fix the smashed window in Missy's bedroom. Later there would be time to deal with the decision of moving from 112 Ocean Avenue.

Upstairs, George had just nailed plywood over the shattered window frame to protect the room from damage by the weather when Kathy called up from the kitchen that his office in Syosset wanted him on the telephone. The company's accountant reminded George that the Internal Revenue Agent was due to come by at noon.

Not wanting to leave the house, George asked the accountant to handle the tax situation himself, but the man refused. It was George's responsibility to determine how to pay the taxes. George hesitated, certain that something would happen if he left. But Kathy signaled that he should go.

After he hung up, Kathy said that the appointment shouldn't take too long. She and Missy would be all right while he was gone. She would call a glazier in Amityville to drive over and fix the broken panes in Missy's window and throughout the house. Meekly, George nodded at his wife's advice, then left for Syosset. Neither had mentioned Jodie's name.

While Kathy was giving Missy her lunch, George Kekoris called. He was sorry he hadn't been able to get there as he'd promised George, but said he felt he'd picked up the flu in Buffalo. Kekoris' bout of illness had forced him to cancel all his appointments for the Psychical Research Institute. He was sure that he'd be fine by the following day, however, and planned to stay at the Lutzes' Wednesday night.

Kathy half-listened to his explanation. She was watching Missy eat. The little girl seemed to be having a secret conversation with someone under the kitchen table. Every once in a while Missy would extend her hand beneath the plastic tablecloth to offer her peanut butter and jelly sandwich. She didn't seem to be aware that her mother was watching her movements.

From her position, Kathy could see there was nothing under the table, but she did want to ask her daughter about Jodie. Finally Kekoris was finished and she hung up.

"Missy," Kathy said, sitting down at the table. "Is Jodie the angel you told me about?"

The little girl looked at her mother, confusion on her face.

"You remember," Kathy continued. "You asked me if angels speak?"

Missy's eyes lit up. "Yes, Mama," she nodded. "Jodie's an angel. He talks to me all the time."

"I don't understand. You've seen pictures of angels. You saw the ones we had on the Christmas tree?"

Missy nodded again.

"You said he's a pig. So how can you say he's an angel?"

Missy's eyebrows grew together as she concentrated. "He says he is, Mama," she nodded her head several times. "He told me."

Kathy hitched her chair closer to Missy. "What does he say when he talks to you?"

Again the little girl seemed confused.

"You know what I mean, Missy," Kathy pressed her daughter. "Do you play games?"

"Oh, no," Missy shook her head. "He tells me about the little boy who used to live in my room." She looked around to see if anybody was listening. "He died, Mama," she whispered. "The little boy got sick and he died."

"I see," Kathy said. "What else did he tell you?"

The little girl thought for a moment. "Last night he said I was going to live here forever so I could play with the little boy."

Horrified, Kathy put her finger to her mouth because she wanted to scream.

George's session with the IRS had not gone well. The agent had disallowed deduction after deduction, and George's only hope lay in the appeal the agent said he could file. It was a temporary reprieve, at least. After the man left, George called Kathy to say that he'd pick up the boys at school on his way home.

When he arrived after three, Kathy and Missy had their coats on. "Don't undress, George," she said. "We're leaving for my mother's right now."

George and the two boys looked at her. "What happened?" he asked.

"Jodie told Missy he's an angel, that's what happened." She began to push the boys out the front door. "We're getting out of here."

George held up his hands. "*Wait* a minute, will you? What do you mean he's an angel?"

Kathy looked down at her daughter. "Missy, tell your father what the pig said."

The little girl nodded. "He said he's an angel, Daddy. He told me."

George was about to ask his daughter another question when he was interrupted by loud barking from behind the house. "Harry!" he cried. "We forgot about Harry!"

When George and the others reached him, Harry was barking furiously at the boathouse, frantically running around his compound and jerking up short every time he reached the end of his steel leash.

"What's the matter, boy?" George said, patting the dog's neck. "Someone in the boathouse?" Harry twisted out of his grasp.

"Don't go in there!" Kathy yelled. "Please! Let's get out of here now!"

George hesitated, then bent down and snapped the leash off Harry's collar. The dog leaped forward with a savage snarl and ran out of his gate. The door to the boathouse was closed and the best Harry could do was leap against it. Again he started his wild barking.

George was all set to unlock the door and fling it open. Instead, Danny and Chris ran past him and leaped on Harry, wrestling the big dog away. "Don't let him go in there!" Danny screamed. "He'll get killed!"

George grabbed Harry's collar and helped pull him down to a sitting position.

"It's all right!" Chris kept assuring the powerful,

agitated animal. "It's all right, boy!" But Harry would not be calmed.

"Let's get him inside the house," George panted. "If he can't see the boathouse, he'll stop!"

As he and the boys were drawing Harry into the house, a van pulled into the driveway. George saw that it was a window repairman. He and Kathy looked at one another. "Oh, my God," Kathy said, "I forgot all about having called him." They hadn't reckoned on this kind of delay.

His pudgy face and broad accent gave away his Slavic descent. "I figured you folks needed the fixing right away," he said, "what with the bad weather we been having. Yah," he continued as he opened his rear doors, "better to fix now. If everything inside get wet because of outside, it cost you more money."

"Okay, that's fine," George said. "Come on in and I'll show you the windows that got busted."

"The wind the other night, yah?" the man asked.

"Yeah, the wind," George answered.

It was almost six P.M. before the man was done. When the new window panes were scraped free of putty, he stepped back to admire his work. "I'm sorry," he said to George, "I could not fix window in little girl's room. You need carpenter first." He gathered up his tools. "You get him, then I come back, yah?"

"Yeah," George nodded. "We'll get him and you can come back." He reached into his pants pocket. "How much do I owe you?"

"No, no," the man protested. "No money now. You neighbor. We send bill, okay?"

"Okay!" George said, relieved. His cash *was* very low at the moment.

Somehow the glazier's kindness and friendliness left

its mark on their spirits that night. After he left, Kathy —who had been sitting in the kitchen with her coat on all the time he worked—suddenly got up and took it off. Without saying a word to George, she began to prepare supper.

"I'm not too hungry," George said. "A grilled cheese sandwich would do just fine."

Kathy took out hamburger meat for herself and the children. As she worked preparing the meal, she kept Danny and Chris with her in the kitchen, insisting they do their homework in the nook. Missy sat in the living room with George, watching television while he built up a fire.

The glazier had been just the reassurance they needed. After all, nothing had happened to *him* while he was in the playroom or the sewing room. The Lutzes realized that maybe their imaginations were too fired up and they were panicking unnecessarily. All thought of abandoning their home had momentarily disappeared.

Father Mancuso was an individual who despised bullies, be they man, animal, or the unknown. The priest felt that the force that had 112 Ocean Avenue in its grip was taking undue advantage of the fears of the Lutzes and of himself. Before he retired Tuesday night, Father Mancuso prayed that this evil force could somehow be reasoned with; that it should know what it was doing was totally insane. How could it derive pleasure from pain, he asked himself? The priest knew there was only one answer—it had to be demonic.

Just to be on the safe side, George and Kathy decided the children should sleep in the master bedroom again. With Harry inside, down in the cellar, Danny, Chris, and Missy were put to bed. George and Kathy made themselves as comfortable as they could: Kathy stretched out on two chairs; George insisted he was all right with one. He told Kathy he planned to stay awake all night and sleep in the morning.

At 3:15 A.M., George heard the marching band strike up downstairs. This time he did not go to investigate. He told himself it was all in his head, and when he went down, there would be nothing to see. So he sat there, watching Kathy and the children, listening as the musicians paraded up and down his living room, horns and drums blasting away loud enough to be heard half a mile away. All during the maddening performance, Kathy and the children did not awaken.

Finally, George must have dozed off in his chair, because Kathy awoke to hear him screaming. He was yelling in two different tongues—languages she had never heard before!

She ran to her husband's chair on the other side of the bed to shake him out of his dream.

George began groaning, and when Kathy touched him, he cried out in another completely different voice: "It's in Chris' room! It's in Chris' room! It's in Chris' room!"

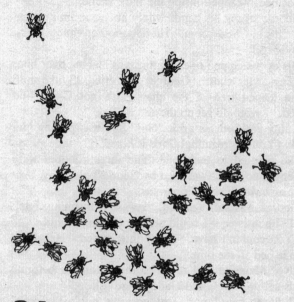

24 January 13 —

George is positive he wasn't dreaming. From his position he was sure he could see clear to the boys' bedroom on the third floor. He had been watching a shadowy figure approach Chris' bed.

He tried to rush to his sleeping son's side and grab him away from the menacing shape. But George couldn't get up from his chair! He was pinned to the seat by a firm hand on his shoulders. It was a struggle George knew he couldn't win.

The shadow hovered over Chris. George, helpless, shouted: "It's in Chris' room!" No one heard him.

"It's in Chris' room!" he repeated. Then the pressure on his shoulders lifted and George felt himself being

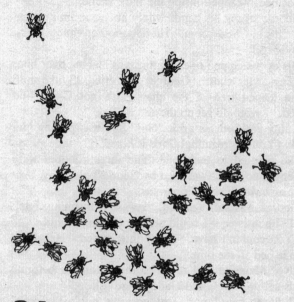233

pushed. His arms came free and he could see Chris was out of bed, wrapped inside the dark shape.

George swung his hands wildly about, again screaming: "It's in Chris' room!" He felt another violent push.

"George!"

His eyes snapped open. Kathy was leaning over him, pushing at his chest. "George!" she cried. "Wake up!"

He leaped free of the chair. "It's got Chris!" he yelled. "I've got to get up there!"

Kathy grabbed his arm. "No!" She was pulling him back. "You're dreaming! Chris is *here*!"

She pointed to their bed. The three children were under the covers. Awakened by George's shouting, they were now watching their parents.

George was still agitated. "I wasn't dreaming, I tell you!" he insisted. "I could see it pick him up and. . . ."

"You couldn't have," Kathy interrupted. "He's been here in bed all the time."

"No, Mama. I had to go to the bathroom before." Chris sat up. "You and Daddy were asleep."

"I never heard you. Did you use my bathroom?" Kathy asked.

"Unh-unh. The door was locked, so I went upstairs."

George went to the bathroom. The door *was* locked.

"Upstairs?" asked Kathy.

"Yeah," Chris answered. "But I got scared."

"Why?" his father asked.

"Because I could look through the floor and see you, Daddy."

The Lutzes remained awake for the rest of the night. Only Missy fell back to sleep. In the morning, George called Father Mancuso.

* * *

Minutes before, Father Mancuso had come to a decision. His anguish over the Lutzes' children and their safety had overcome his fear. Feeling he had been a coward long enough, Father Mancuso was now resolved to return to the Bishop and ask that he be allowed to continue communicating with George.

He showered for the first time in days, then prepared to shave. As he was plugging in his electric razor, Father Mancuso gasped. Beneath his eyes were the same black circles he had first seen at his mother's. The telephone rang at that very moment.

Even before he answered the telephone, the priest knew who was calling.

"Yes, George?" he said.

George was too preoccupied to notice that Father Mancuso had anticipated him. He announced that he and Kathy had decided to take the Chancellors' advice and leave 112 Ocean Avenue. They were going to his mother-in-law's until George could get some kind of investigation going. Too many incidents were beginning to involve the children, and George felt that if he delayed any longer, Danny, Chris, and Missy might be in frightful danger.

The priest did not ask what kinds of incidents, nor did he mention the reappearance of the circles under his eyes. He readily agreed the children's welfare should be everyone's prime concern and that George was right about going. "Let whatever's there have the place," he said. "Just go."

Danny and Chris did not go to school in Amityville that morning. Kathy kept them home again because she wanted to pack as soon as possible. George said they'd leave as soon as he called the police to tell them the family would be away for a while. He also wanted them to have Mrs. Conners' telephone number in case of any emergency. But when he picked up the telephone to dial the Police Department, the line was dead.

When her husband told Kathy the phone was out of order, she became extremely nervous. Hurriedly she dressed the children and then, without taking a change of clothes, herded them out to the van.

George brought Harry from the cellar and put him in the rear of the van. Then he went around the house and checked to make sure all the doors were locked. Finishing with the boathouse, George climbed behind the wheel of the van. He turned the ignition key but the motor wouldn't turn over.

"George?" Kathy's voice quivered. "What's wrong?"

"Take it easy," he said. "We got enough gas. Let me take a look under the hood."

As he got out of the van, he looked up at the sky. The clouds had grown dark and menacing. George felt a cold wind picking up. By the time he lifted the hood, the first raindrops were hitting the windshield.

George never got a good look at what could have caused the van to stall. A huge gust of wind blew in from the Amityville River in the back of the house, and the hood was slammed down. George had just leaped aside to avoid the falling metal when a lightning bolt struck behind the garage. The clap of thunder was almost instantaneous, and the clouds broke in a solid sheet of water that drenched George immediately.

He ran for the front door and unlocked it. "Get in!" he shouted to his family in the van. Kathy and the children bolted for the open door, but by the time he managed to close it behind them, all were soaking wet.

We're trapped, he thought to himself, not daring to voice the thought to Kathy. It's not going to let us go.

The rains and wind picked up in intensity, and by one o'clock in the afternoon, Amityville was hit by another storm of hurricane strength. At three, the electricity went out, but fortunately the heat remained in the house. George switched on the portable radio in the kitchen. The weather report said it was 20 degrees and that sleet was pelting all of Long Island. Since the radar showed an enormous low pressure system covering the entire metropolitan area, the weatherman could not predict when the storm would subside.

George dealt with Missy's broken window as best he could, shoving towels into the spaces where it hung away from the frame, then nailing an old blanket over the entire window. Before he had finished, his fresh dry clothes were soaked again.

In the kitchen, George looked at the thermometer that hung beside the back door. It read 80 degrees and the house was getting uncomfortably warm. He knew that with the electricity off, the oil burner's thermostat wouldn't operate. But when George looked again at the thermometer, it was up to 85 degrees.

To cool off the house, George had to have some fresh air. He inched open the windows on the enclosed porch —the only room that faced away from the storm's main onslaught.

From the time the storm broke, it had remained dark outside, and even though it was daytime, Kathy had lit candles. At four-thirty it was as if night had already settled over 112 Ocean Avenue.

Every once in a while she would pick up the telephone to see if it was working again, but she really had little hope that it would be—the storm would prevent any repair crews from going out on call. The children weren't fazed at all by the darkness. They treated the whole affair as a holiday, noisily running up and down the staircase, playing hide-and-seek. Since the boys were much better at hiding themselves, Missy was usually "it." Harry happily joined in the romping, finally irritating George to the point where he cuffed the dog with a newspaper. Harry ran off and hid behind Kathy.

By six in the evening, the storm still hadn't slackened. It was as though all the water in the world was being dumped on top of 112 Ocean Avenue. And inside the house, the temperature was up to 90 degrees. George went to the basement to look at the oil burner. It *was* off, but it didn't matter; the heat continued to rise in all the rooms except Missy's.

Desperate, he decided to make a final appeal to God. Holding a candle, George began going from room to room, asking the Lord to send away whoever didn't belong there. He felt mildly reassured when there was no sinister reaction to his prayers.

After the playroom door had been damaged during the first storm, George had removed the lock. Now as he approached the room to recite his appeal to God, he saw the green slime was back, leaking from the open hole in the door and oozing onto the floor of the hallway. George watched as the pool of jelly-like substance slowly wound its way toward the staircase.

He pulled off the pine boards nailed across the door and threw it open, half-expecting to find the room filled with the slimy material. But its only source seemed to be the empty lock hole in the door!

George gathered some towels from the third floor bathroom and stuffed them into the opening. The towels soon became saturated, but the jelly stopped flowing. He wiped up the slime that had accumulated in the hallway and had managed to flow down the steps. George had no intention of telling his wife about this latest discovery.

All the time her husband was going through the house, Kathy sat by the telephone. She had tried opening the kitchen door a little to let in some air, but even when it was only slightly ajar, rainwater showered into the room. She began to doze from the oppressive heat.

When George finally returned to the kitchen, she was almost fast asleep, resting her head on her arms on the breakfast table in the nook. Kathy was perspiring, the back of her neck damp to his touch. When he tried to awaken her, she lifted her head slightly, mumbled something he couldn't understand, then let her forehead fall back on her arms.

George had no need to check whether the rain and windstorm had let up. Torrents of water were still smashing against the house, and he somehow knew they wouldn't be allowed to leave 112 Ocean Avenue that night. He picked Kathy up in his arms and took her to their bedroom, noting the time on the kitchen clock. It was exactly 8 P.M.

Finally the 90 degree heat got to Danny, Chris, and Missy. Their running about the house most of the day had worn them out, so shortly after George had taken Kathy upstairs, they were ready for bed. George was surprised to find it was somewhat cooler in the boys' room on the third floor. He knew that hot air rises, and on the top floor it should have been well above ninety.

Missy sleepily climbed into bed beside Kathy, but refused to be covered with a sheet or blanket. Before George went back downstairs, she and the boys were asleep.

George and Harry were now all alone in the living room. For a change, the dog didn't seem to be about to fall asleep early but watched his owner's every move. He, too, was suffering from the excessive heat. Whenever George rose from his chair to go into another room, Harry would not follow, but remained stretched out in the cool draft beneath the living room windows.

George thought of running outside to the van to see if it would start. It was still standing in the driveway and George knew its engine would probably be wet by now. But the real deterrent was George's suspicion that once he left, he might not be able to get back into the house. Something within him warned him that he'd never get the front or kitchen door open again.

Suddenly, at ten o'clock, the 90 degree heat began to break. Harry noticed it first. The dog stood, sniffed the air, then walked over to the unlit fireplace where George was sitting, and whimpered. His pathetic sounds broke his master's concentration on the van. George looked up and shivered. There was a definite drop in the house's temperature.

A half hour later, the thermometer read 60 degrees. George started for the basement to get some logs. Harry trotted along behind him to the cellar door, but would not descend the steps with George. He remained in the open doorway, constantly turning his head as if to see if someone was coming up behind him.

George used his flashlight to search out every corner of the basement, but there were no signs of anything unusual. With several logs in his arms, George climbed back upstairs and tried the telephone in the kitchen. It was still dead. He was all set to relight the kindling wood in the fireplace when he thought he heard Missy cry out.

When he reached his bedroom, the little girl was shivering; he had forgotten to cover her when the house got chilly. Kathy, on her stomach, was sleeping like a drugged person, not moving or turning in bed. George also tucked blankets about his wife's cool body.

When he finally went back down to the living room, George decided not to make a fire. He wanted to be free to stay near Kathy and the children. Tonight, he thought, I'd better be ready for anything. George put on Harry's long metal leash and took the dog up to the master bedroom. He left the door open, but knotted the leash so that Harry blocked the doorway completely. Then George kicked off his shoes, and without undressing, slid into bed beside Missy and Kathy. Rather than lie down, he sat up with his back resting against the headboard.

At one o'clock, George felt he was freezing. Because of the noise of the raging storm outside, he knew there was no hope of heat in the house that night from the oil burner. He began to weep to himself about the sorry plight he and his family were in. He now realized he should have fled when Father Mancuso originally warned him. "Oh, God, help us," he moaned.

Suddenly, Kathy lifted up her head. While he watched, she got off the bed and turned to look into the mirror on the wall. George saw in the candlelight that her eyes were open, but he knew she was still asleep.

Kathy stared at her reflection for a moment, then turned away from the mirrored wall and started for the bedroom door. But she stopped when she came to an obstacle: Harry was fast asleep, stretched across the threshold, blocking her path.

George leaped from the bed and seized his wife. Kathy looked at him with unseeing eyes. To George, she seemed to be in a trance.

"Kathy!" he cried. "Wake up!" When George shook her, there was no response or reaction. Then her eyes closed. Kathy went limp in his arms and gently he half-pulled, half-lifted her back to the bed. First he sat Kathy down, then straightened her legs so that she was lying flat. Her trance-like state seemed to affect her whole body. She was like a rag doll.

George noted that Missy, in the middle of the bed, had slept through the whole episode. But then his attention was diverted by a movement in the doorway. He saw Harry struggle to his feet, shake violently, and then begin to retch. The dog threw up all over the floor, but kept gagging and trying to force out something that seemed stuck in his throat. Restricted by his leash, the poor dog was only twisting the chain more tightly about his writhing body.

The odor of vomit caused George to gag too. He fled into the bathroom, gulped a mouthful of water, took a deep breath, and came out with towels from the rack. After he mopped up the floor, George untied Harry and set the dog free. Harry looked up at George, wagged his tail several times, then stretched himself out on the floor of the hallway, closing his eyes. "There's not much wrong with you now," George whispered under his breath.

He listened, but everything was quiet throughout the house—*much* too quiet. In a few moments, George realized the storm had stopped. There was no rain, no wind. The stillness was so complete it was as though someone had turned off running water in a sink. There was a vacuum of silence at 112 Ocean Avenue.

With the storm gone, the temperature outside began to drop and in a very short time, the house became ice cold. George could feel the bedroom become even chillier than it had been. He still had all his clothes on when he slipped back beneath the covers.

There was a noise above George's head. He looked up and listened. Something was scraping along the floor of the boys' bedroom. The noise became louder, and George could tell the movement was faster now. The boys' beds were sliding back and forth!

George managed to throw off his covers, but he could not lift his body out of bed. There was no pressure as there had been before when he sat in the bedroom chair. George just didn't have the strength to move!

Now he heard the dresser drawers across his room begin to open and close. A candle was still on his night-stand and he could make out the drawers rapidly sliding back and forth. One drawer would fly open, then another, then the first would bang shut. Tears of frustration and fear flooded George's eyes.

Almost immediately after that, the voices began. He could hear them downstairs, but couldn't make out what was being said. He only knew that it sounded as if a lot of people were thronging on the first floor. George's head began to roll as he tried to reach over and touch Missy or Kathy.

Then the marching band struck up downstairs, its music drowning out the unintelligible voices. George thought he must be in a madhouse. He could distinctly hear musicians parade around the entire first floor—and then their first steps as they began to mount the staircase!

George was screaming now, but he heard no sounds coming from his throat. His body whipped back and forth on the bed and he could feel the terrible strain on his neck muscles as he vainly tried to lift his head from the mattress. Finally George gave up. He realized the mattress was soaking wet.

The beds were banging around above George's head, and the dresser drawers in his room were flying back and forth as the band headed up the steps to the second floor. But that was not all. Despite all the noise, George now heard doors throughout the house beginning to slam back and forth!

He saw the door to the bedroom swing wildly as though someone were yanking it open and then immediately slamming it shut. George could also see Harry lying outside in the hallway, completely undisturbed by the racket. Either that dog is drugged, George thought, or I'm the one who's going mad!

A terrible, blinding flash of lightning lit up the bedroom. George heard the thunderbolt strike something close outside. Then there was a smashing blow that shook the entire house. The storm was back, with torrents of rain and wind lashing 112 Ocean Avenue from top to bottom.

George lay there panting, his heart thumping loudly in his chest. He was waiting, knowing something else was about to happen. Then George let out a horrible, silent scream. Somebody was on the bed with him!

He felt himself being stepped on! Strong, heavy feet struck his legs and body. George shut his eyes. He could feel the pain from the blows. Oh God! he thought. They're hooves. It's an animal!

George must have passed out from fright, because the next thing he remembers was the sight of Danny and Chris standing beside his bed. "Daddy, Daddy, wake up!" they were crying, "there's something in our room!"

He blinked his eyes. In a glance he saw it was light outside. The storm had stopped. The dresser drawers were all open, and his two sons were pleading with him to get up.

Missy! Kathy! George turned to look at them. They were still next to him, both still sound asleep. He turned back to the boys, who were trying to pull him out of bed. "What's the matter?" he asked. "What's in your room?"

"It's a monster!" Danny cried. "He doesn't have any face!"

"It tried to grab us," Chris broke in, "but we ran away! Come on, Daddy, get up!"

George tried. He almost got his head off the mattress when he heard Harry bark furiously. George looked past the boys through the open doorway. The dog was standing in the hallway, snarling and growling at the staircase. Even though he was unleashed, Harry did not head for the stairs, but continued to crouch in the hallway, teeth bared, barking at something or someone George couldn't see from his position on the bed.

With a tremendous burst of determination, George finally heaved his whole body off the mattress. He arose so suddenly that he crashed into Danny and Chris. Then he ran for the open door and looked up at the steps.

On the top step stood a gigantic figure in white. George knew it was the hooded image Kathy had first glimpsed in the fireplace. The being was pointing at him!

George whirled and raced back into the bedroom, grabbed up Missy, and shoved her into Danny's arms. "Take her outside!" he shouted. "You go with them, Chris!"

Then he bent over Kathy and lifted her off the bed.

"Hurry!" George yelled after the boys. Then he too ran from the room, Harry following him down the steps.

On the first floor, George saw the front door was open, hanging from its hinges again, torn away by some powerful force.

Danny, Chris, and Missy were outside. The little girl, just awakening, was squirming in her brother's arms. Not knowing where she was, she started to cry with fright.

George ran for the van. He put Kathy on the front seat and then helped the children into the rear. Harry jumped in behind them, and he slammed the door on Kathy's side. George ran around to the other side of the vehicle, jumped in the driver's seat, and prayed.

He jammed in the ignition key.

The motor turned over immediately.

Spraying wet gravel, George backed out of the driveway. When he hit the street, he skidded, spun the wheel, and stepped on the gas at the same time. The van teetered for a moment, then all four tires grabbed and smoke shot up from the rubber treads. In another instant, the van was tearing up Ocean Avenue.

As he steered the van toward safety, George looked into the side view mirror. His house was fast disappearing from his sight. "Thank God!" he muttered to himself. "I'll never see you again, you sonofabitch!"

It was seven o'clock on the morning of January 14, 1976; the twenty-eighth day the Lutzes had lived in 112 Ocean Avenue.

25 January 15 — That morning, at the very
moment the Lutzes were fleeing from their home, Father
Mancuso decided to get out of town.

He waited until eleven o'clock, because then it would
be eight A.M. in San Francisco, and he didn't want to
awaken his cousin too early with a telephone call. The
priest announced he was flying West for a vacation. He
would leave in a day or so, probably on Friday, January 16.

Father Mancuso hung up, feeling greatly relieved.
This was the first positive step he had taken in weeks.
The priest reasoned that a week in the California sun

could only help his run-down condition and possibly bake the flu out of his system. Let the diabolical powers in 112 Ocean Avenue have the house and the cruel New York winter weather!

He called his office back at the diocese in order to inform them of his plans. They were to reschedule his appointments and duties until after January 30th. He would contact some of his clients in counseling on his own.

As the morning wore on, the priest felt progressively better. He had much to do before leaving, and all his thoughts of the Lutzes were shunted into the background. But at four in the afternoon, George Lutz called from his mother-in-law's in East Babylon. He said he wanted to let Father Mancuso know that he, Kathy, and the children were going to stay there until the scientific investigations were made at his house in Amityville.

"That's fine, George," Father Mancuso said. "But be careful of who goes into the house. Don't make a circus out of this thing."

"Oh, I won't, Father," George replied. "We don't want people trampling all over the place. All our stuff is still there. Nobody gets in unless I say so."

"Good," the priest said. "Just follow up on the parapsychologists. The Chancery says they're the best equipped to investigate a situation like this."

"There's just one thing," George broke in. "Supposing they can't come up with answers. And after last night, Father, I frankly don't think they can. Then what? What happens next?"

Father Mancuso let out a gasp. "What do you mean, *after last night*? Don't tell me you stayed there again?"

There was silence on the telephone. Finally George

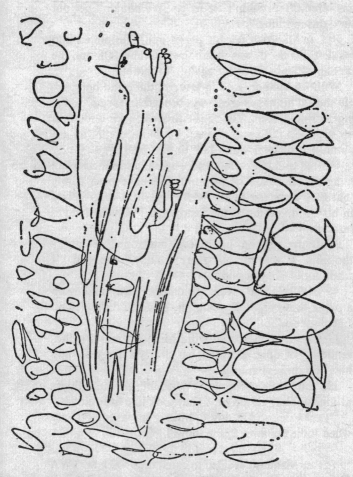

Missy's picture of "Jodie" running through the snow

answered. "It wouldn't let us go. We couldn't get out until this morning."

Father Mancuso felt his palms itch. He looked into his left hand. It was becoming blotchy. Oh no, he thought. Please God, not again! No more!

Without another word to George, the priest hung up. He shoved his hands crossways beneath his armpits, trying to shield them. He began to rock back and forth on his heels. "Please, please," he whimpered, "let me alone. I promise I won't talk to him again."

George couldn't understand why Father Mancuso had hung up on him. The priest should have been happy that they were out of the house. He held the receiver in his hand, staring at the instrument. "What'd I say?" he murmured.

A sharp tug on his sleeve interrupted George's thoughts. It was Missy. "Here, Daddy," she said. "I made Jodie like you said."

"What?" George asked. His daughter was holding up a paper drawing. "Oh, yeah," he said. "Jodie's picture. Let me see it."

George took the paper from Missy. It was a child's rendering of a pig, distorted, but clearly a five-year-old's idea of a running animal.

He raised his eyebrows. "What are all these things around Jodie?" he asked. "They look like little clouds."

"That's snow, Daddy," Missy answered. "That's when Jodie ran away in the snow."

Father Mancuso decided to catch the 9:00 P.M. TWA flight to San Francisco. When the panic after George's call had left him, the priest immediately picked up the telephone and spoke to his cousin's wife. He told her he had changed his mind and would be coming out that night. She agreed to meet him at San Francisco's International Airport.

Father Mancuso packed only one suitcase; called his mother, the diocese office, and a cab company. By eight, he was out of the Rectory and on his way to Kennedy Airport. When the priest checked in at the TWA counter he looked again at his palms. The blotches were gone, but his fear wasn't.

Jimmy and Carey went to stay at her mother's house that night. But before they left, there was a small celebration at Mrs. Conners' house. Because of the dramatic feeling of relief that swept over the Lutzes just to be free of 112 Ocean Avenue, it was practically a party.

George and Kathy now wanted to talk about their experiences, and in her family, they had a sympathetic and credulous audience. Events spilled from their lips in a flood as they tried to explain what had happened to them. Finally, George revealed his plans to rid his house of whatever evil force remained there. He told his mother-in-law and Jimmy that research groups would be invited to participate, but they would have to conduct their investigations by themselves. Under no circumstances would he or Kathy ever enter 112 Ocean Avenue again.

Danny, Chris, and Missy were to sleep in Jimmy's room. The boys were exhausted from the harrowing appearance of the "monster" the night before and from the excitement of fleeing to their grandmother's. But they didn't want to talk about the white-hooded demon figure. When George pressed them to tell their version, both boys fell silent and looks of fear came over their faces.

Missy appeared to be entirely unaffected by the whole affair. She adapted easily enough to the new adventure and made herself right at home with a few dolls she had cached at her grandmother's. She wasn't even perturbed when Kathy questioned her further about Jodie's picture. The little girl would say only, "That is what the pig looked like."

George and Kathy took their baths early. Both luxuriated in the hot water and soaked for a long time. It was a dual cleansing: their bodies and their fright. By ten P.M., they were in bed in the guest room. For the first time in almost a month, the Lutzes fell asleep in each other's arms.

George awoke first. He felt as if he was having a dream, because he had the sensation of floating in air!

He was aware of his body being flown around the bedroom and then landing softly back on the bed. Then, still in his dreamlike state, George saw Kathy levitate off the bed. She rose about a foot and slowly began to drift away from him.

George reached out a hand to his wife. In his eyes, the movement was almost in slow motion, as though his arm was not attached to his body. He tried to call to her, but for some reason, he couldn't remember her name. George could only watch Kathy fly higher toward the ceiling. Then he felt himself being lifted, and again he had the sensation of floating.

He could hear someone calling to him from a great distance. George knew the voice. It sounded very familiar. He heard his name again. "George?"

Now he remembered. It was Kathy. George looked down and saw she was back on the bed, looking up at him.

He began to drift toward Kathy, then felt himself

slowly settling back down on the bed beside her. "George!" she cried. "You were floating in the air!"

Kathy grabbed his arm and pulled him off the bed. "Come on!" she shouted. "We've got to get out of this room!"

As though he was sleepwalking, George followed his wife. At the head of the staircase they both stopped and recoiled in horror. Coming *up* the steps toward them was a snake-like line of greenish-black slime!

George knew he had not been dreaming. It was all real. Whatever he had thought they had left forever back at 112 Ocean Avenue was following them—wherever the Lutzes fled.

EPILOGUE

On February 18, 1976, Marvin Scott of New York's Channel 5 decided to investigate further the reports on the so-called cursed home of Amityville, Long Island. The mission called for spending the night in the haunted home at 112 Ocean Avenue. Psychics, clairvoyants, a demonologist, and parapsychologists were invited to participate.

Scott had originally contacted the recent tenants, the Lutz family, and requested permission to film activities at their deserted house. George Lutz agreed and sat down at a meeting with Scott in a small pizzeria in Amityville. George refused to re-enter 112 Ocean

Avenue, but said he and his wife, Kathy, would wait for the investigators the next day at the Italian restaurant.

To provoke the overpowering force said to be within the house, a crucifix and blessed candles were placed in the center of the dining room table.

The researchers held the first of three seances at 10:30 P.M. Present around the table were Lorraine Warren, a clairvoyant; her husband, Ed, a demonologist; psychics Mary Pascarella and Mrs. Albert Riley; and George Kekoris of the Psychical Research Institute in Durham, North Carolina. Marvin Scott also joined the group at the table.

During the seance, Mary Pascarella became ill and had to leave the room. In a quaking voice, she said, "that in back of everything there seems to be some kind of black shadow that forms a head, and it moves. And as it moves, I feel personally threatened."

Mrs. Riley, in a mediumistic trance, began gasping. "It's upstairs in the bedroom. What's here makes your heart speed up. My heart's pounding." Ed Warren wanted to end the seance. Mrs. Riley continued to gasp, then quickly came out of her trance and back to normal consciousness.

Then George Kekoris, the psychic researcher, also became violently ill and had to leave the table. Observer Mike Linder of WNEW-FM stated that he had felt a sudden numbness, a kind of cold sensation.

Clairvoyant Lorraine Warren finally voiced her own opinion: "Whatever is here is, in my estimation, most definitely of a negative nature. It has nothing to do with anyone who had once walked the earth in human form. It is right from the bowels of the earth."

Television cameraman Steve Petropolis, who had been assigned some scary assignments in combat zones, experienced heart palpitations and shortness of breath when he investigated the sewing room upstairs where the negative force was said to be concentrated. When Lorraine Warren and Marvin Scott went into that room, they both came out saying that they had felt a momentary chill.

Lorraine and Ed Warren also found a source of discomfort in the living room. Mrs. Warren thought some negative forces were centered in statues and nonliving things: "That whatever is here, is able to move around at will. It doesn't have to stay here, but I think it's a resting place." She also thought there was something demonic in the inanimate objects. Mrs. Warren indicated the fireplace and banister on the second floor, without being forewarned of their connection with the Lutzes' problems.

As some people slept in some of the second floor bedrooms, a photographer shot infrared pictures in the vain hope of capturing some ghostly image on film. Jerry Solfvin of the Psychical Research Institute wandered about the house with a battery lantern, searching for physical evidence.

At 3:30 A.M., the Warrens attempted another seance. There was nothing unusual reported, no sounds or strange phenomena. All the psychics felt the room had been neutralized. The atmosphere, they said, simply wasn't right at the moment. But they definitely felt that the house on Ocean Avenue was harboring a demonic spirit, one that could be removed only by an exorcist.

When Marvin Scott returned to the little pizzeria, the Lutzes were gone. By March, they had moved clear across the country to California. They left behind all their belongings, all their worldly goods, and all the money they had invested in their dream home. Just to be rid of the place, they signed their interest over to the bank that held the mortgage. Pending its resale, its windows were boarded up to discourage vandalism and to prevent the curious, the morbid, and the warned from entering.

On Good Friday, 1976, Father Frank Mancuso recovered from pneumonia, and in April, he was transferred by the Bishop of his diocese to another parish. It is nowhere near 112 Ocean Avenue.

Now, Missy gets upset when she is asked about Jodie; Danny and Chris can still vividly describe the "monster" who chased them that final night, and Kathy will not talk about that period in her life at all. George has sold his interest in William H. Parry, Inc. He does hope that those who hear his story will understand how dangerous negative entities can be to the unwary—to the unbelieving. "They *are* real," George insists, "and they do inflict evil when the opportunity presents itself."

AFTERWORD:
A Note From the Author

To the extent that I can verify them, all the events in this book are true. George Lee and Kathleen Lutz undertook the exhaustive and frequently painful task of reconstructing their twenty-eight days in the house in Amityville on a tape recorder, refreshing each other's memories so that the final oral "diary" would be as complete as possible. Not only did George and Kathy agree on virtually every detail they had both experienced, many of their impressions and reports were later substantiated by the testimony of independent witnesses such as Father Mancuso and local police officials. But perhaps the most telling evidence in support of their story is circumstantial—it takes more than imagination or a case of "nerves" to drive a normal, healthy family of five to the drastic step of suddenly abandoning a desirable three-story house, complete with finished basement, swimming pool, and boathouse, without even pausing to take along their personal household belongings.

I should point out, too, that when the Lutzes fled their home in early 1976, they had no thought of putting their experiences into book form. Only after the press and broadcast media began issuing reports on the house that the Lutzes considered distorted and sensationalized did they consent to have their story published. Nor were they aware that so many of their claims would be corroborated by others. In addition to checking their tape recordings for internal consistency, I conducted my own personal interviews with others involved in the case; and indeed, George and Kathy did not learn of Father Mancuso's tribulations until this book's final draft was written.

Before they had moved into their new home, the Lutzes were far from being experts on the subject of psychic phenomena. As far as they can recall, the only books they'd read that might be even remotely considered "occult" were a few popular works on Transcendental Meditation. But as I've since discovered by talking with those familiar with parapsychology, almost every one of their claims bears a strong parallel to other reports of hauntings, psychic "invasions" and the like that have been published over the years in a wide variety of sources. For example:

*The chilling cold that George and others noted is a syndrome repeatedly reported by visitors to haunted houses who sense a "cold spot" or pervasive chill. (Occulists speculate that a disembodied entity may draw on thermal energy and body heat to gain the power it needs to become visible and move objects.)

*Animals are often said to display discomfort and even terror in haunted surroundings. This was certainly true of Harry, the family dog, to say nothing of human visitors who had never entered the house before— Kathy's aunt, a neighbor's boy, and others.

*The window that slammed on Danny's hand has its echo in an English case in which a car door closed by itself, crushing the hand of a woman who was arriving to investigate paranormal reports. Minutes later, during the drive to the nearest hospital, her hand reportedly returned to its uninjured state.

*George's visionary glimpse of what he would later identify as Ronnie DeFeo's face, his repeated awakening at the time of the DeFeo murders, and Kathy's dreams of illicit lovemaking have their counterparts in a phenomenon called *retrocognition*, in which an emotionally-charged site apparently manages to transmit images of its past to later visitors.

*The damage to doors, windows and banister, the movement and possible teleportation of the ceramic lion, the nauseating stench in the basement and Rectory are all familiar elements to readers of the voluminous literature about poltergeists or "noisy ghosts," whose behavior has been documented by professional investigators. The "marching band," too, is characteristic of the poltergeist, which is often reported to create dramatically loud noises. (One victim reported the sound of "a grand piano falling downstairs," but with no visible cause or damage.)

Most poltergeist manifestations are said to occur in the presence of a child—usually a girl—approaching puberty. Here, none of the Lutz children seems to have been old enough to serve as the trigger; moreover, most poltergeist antics seem childishly malicious, rather than vicious or physically harmful. But on the other hand, as Father Nicola points out in his *Demonical Possession and Exorcism*, poltergeists sometimes serve as the first manifestation of an entity ultimately bent on demonic possesssion. The inverted crucifix in Kathy's closet, the recurrent flies, and odors of human excrement are all characteristic trademarks of demonic infestation.

What, then, are we to make of the Lutzes' account? There is simply too much independent corroboration of their narrative to support the speculation that they either imagined or fabricated these events. But if the case unfolded as I've reconstructed it here, how are we to interpret it?

What follows is one interpretation, the analysis of an experienced researcher into paranormal phenomena:

"The Lutz home seems to have harbored at least three separate entities. Francine, the medium, sensed at least two ordinary 'ghosts,' that is, earthbound spirits of humans who—for whatever reasons—remain attached to a particular locale long after their physical death and usually want no more than to be left alone to enjoy the spot they've become accustomed to while on earth. The woman whose touch and perfume were perceived by Kathy (Francine cited 'an old woman') may have been that house's original tenant, who only wanted to reassure the new young woman who found 'her' kitchen such an attractive, pleasant spot.

"Similarly, the little boy independently spoken of by Missy and by Kathy's sister-in-law would probably also have been an earth-bound spirit who—again according to mediums and spiritualists—may not have realized he was dead. Lonely and confused in the timeless world of after-death, he would naturally have gravitated to Missy's room, where he was surprised to find her bed occupied by Carey and Jimmy. But if he asked Carey for 'help,' it was evidently not *he* who was arranging for Missy to become his permanent playmate.

"Rather, the hooded figure and 'Jodie the pig' seem to represent a wholly different class of being. Orthodox demonologists believe that fallen angels can manifest themselves as animals or as awe-inspiring human figures at will; therefore, these two apparitions may have been one and the same. Although George saw the eyes of a pig and hoofprints in the snow, Jodie *spoke* with Missy and thus was no mere animal ghost. And the entity who burned its visage into the fireplace wall and dominated the hallway on that final morning may have simply taken a less frightening shape to converse telepathically with a little girl.

"It seems logical that this entity—together with the voices that ordered Father Mancuso to depart and George and Kathy to stop their impromptu exorcism— may have been 'invited in' during the course of occult ceremonies performed in the basement, or on the house's original site. Once established, they would naturally resist any attempts to dislodge them, and with greater vigor than any ordinary ghost would normally display.

"George and Kathy's inexplicable trances, mood changes, repeated levitations, odd dreams, physical transformations can all be read as symptoms of incipient possession. Some who believe in reincarnation say that we pay for past errors by being reborn in a new body and experiencing the consequences of our actions.

But any entity as resolutely malevolent as the ones who tormented the Lutzes would have realized that a return to the flesh might entail retribution in the shape of physical deformity, illness, suffering, and other 'bad Karma.' Thus a particularly nasty spirit might avoid rebirth entirely, instead seizing the bodies of the *living* in order to experience food, sex, alcohol, and other earthly pleasures.

"Evidently George Lutz was not the ideally passive 'horse' for a discarnate rider; the threat to his wife and children galvanized him to fight back. But neither were his unseen adversaries mere ordinary 'ha'nts.' Their unusual strength is suggested by their long-range attacks on Father Mancuso's car, health, and rooms, and by George and Kathy's levitation even after they had fled to her mother's. But why, then, have the Lutzes reported no further trouble after moving to California?

"Another old occult tradition—that spirits cannot extend their power across water—may have some significance here. During the preparation of this book, one of those primarily responsible for it reported feeling weak and nauseous upon sitting down to work on the manuscript—*whenever he did so in his office on Long Island*. But while doing the same task in Manhattan, across the East River, he experienced no ill effects at all."

We're not obliged, of course, to accept this or any other "psychic" interpretation of the events that took place in the house in Amityville. Yet any other hypothesis immediately involves us in trying to construct an even more incredible series of bizarre coincidences, shared hallucinations, and grotesque misinterpretations of fact. It would be helpful if we could duplicate, as in a controlled laboratory experiment, some of the events the Lutzes experienced. But of course we cannot. Disembodied spirits—if they exist—presumably feel no obligation to perform instant replays before the cameras and recording equipment of earnest researchers.

There is no evidence that any strange events occurred at 112 Ocean Avenue after the period of time reported in this book, but this too, makes sense: more than one parapsychologist has noted that occult manifestations—especially those with poltergeist overtones—very often end as suddenly as they began, never to reoccur. And even traditional ghost-hunters assure their clients that structural changes in a house, even a simple rearrangement of furniture, such as would be effected by a new tenant, will bring a speedy end to reports of the abnormal.

As for George and Kathleen Lutz, of course, their curiosity has been more than satisfied. But the rest of us are left with a dilemma: The more "rational" the explanation, the less tenable it becomes. And what I have called *The Amityville Horror* remains one of those dark mysteries that challenges our conventional accounting of what this world contains.

ABOUT THE AUTHOR

JAY ANSON began as a copy boy on the *N.Y. Evening Journal* in 1937, and later worked in advertising and publicity. With over 500 documentary scripts for television to his credit, he is now associated with Professional Films, Inc., and lives in New York City.

We Deliver!

And So Do These Bestsellers.

Bantam Book Catalog

Here's your up-to-the-minute listing of over 1,400 titles by your favorite authors.

This illustrated, large format catalog gives a description of each title. For your convenience, it is divided into categories in fiction and non-fiction—gothics, science fiction, westerns, mysteries, cookbooks, mysticism and occult, biographies, history, family living, health, psychology, art.

So don't delay—take advantage of this special opportunity to increase your reading pleasure.

Just send us your name and address and 50¢ (to help defray postage and handling costs).

BANTAM BOOKS, INC.
Dept. FC, 414 East Golf Road, Des Plaines, Ill. 60016

Mr./Mrs./Miss_____
　　　　　　　　　　(please print)

Address_____

City_____State_____Zip_____

Do you know someone who enjoys books? Just give us their names and addresses and we'll send them a catalog too!

_____

Mr./Mrs./Miss_____

Address_____

City_____State_____Zip_____

_____

Mr./Mrs./Miss_____

Address_____

City_____State_____Zip_____

FC—9/78